Copyright Notice

Copyright © 2012 by Charlie Valentino. All Rights Reserved.

Reproduction or translation of any part of this work beyond that permitted by section 107 or 108 of the 1976 United States Copyright Act without permission of the copyright owner is unlawful. Requests for permission or further information should be addressed to the author.

Charlie Valentino
UK
www.howtopickupwomen.org

This publication is designed to provide accurate and authoritative information in regard to the subject matter covered. It is sold the understanding that the publisher is not engaged in rendering legal, accounting, or other professional services. If legal advice or other expert assistance is required, the services of a competent professional person should be sought.

First Printing, 2012
ISBN-13: 978-1481077934
ISBN-10: 1481077937

Printed in the United States of America

Table of Contents

Part 1 – Introduction	1
Alpha Males - An Evolutionary Look	6
Part 2 - Alpha Male Elements	11
Alpha Male Traits and Characteristics	12
Alpha Element # 1 - Physical Attraction	15
Alpha Element # 2 – Confidence	29
Alpha Element # 3 – Ambition	54
Alpha Element # 4 - Displays of Expertise	63
Alpha Element # 5 - Social Proof	67
Alpha Element # 6 – Leadership	76
Alpha Element # 7 - Ability to Connect	81
Alpha Element # 8 - Life Experiences	95
Part 3 - Alpha Extras	99
Be On A Pedestal	100
Raise Your Social Standards	113
Spotting If Women Like You	119
Quick Fire Questions	125

Conclusion	129
Also By Charlie Valentino	131

Part 1

Introduction

When I was in my late teens, the time I should have been having the time of my life, I was the guy in my group who faded into the background. It didn't help that some of the other guys I hung out with were actually quite big personalities. Looking back, it didn't help either that I saw myself as the better looking guy out of the four of us. This meant that I would put all my faith in my "looks" rather than in developing my personality.

It wasn't until my mid 20's that I realised, finally that looks don't count for as much as you'd believe. Being men, the main thing we go for in women is looks, but it took me too long to realise the same thing wasn't the case with women.

There were many times when my group had girls hanging around. They were often attractive girls too. But surprisingly back then, they never once chose to date the good looking guy who stared at the ground when he spoke. They instead always went for Chris the bad boy, Jimmy the funny guy or Matt the alpha male.

Looking back, I can see the qualities Matt had and what made him attractive to girls in their teens and early twenties. I can see what he was doing right and even some of the things he was doing wrong. I also know exactly what I could have been doing to improve my situation.

When I was seventeen, my college lecturer noticed how I would cover my eyes with my hair so I didn't have to look anybody in the face. When I was seventeen I was denied a job on the grounds that the angry people on the phone might "destroy me." When I was eighteen I bought my first car in the belief that finally that would help me to become more popular with girls. When I was twenty two, I would hide in the toilets at university and wait for everybody to enter the lecture theatre so I could creep in behind everybody else without being seen. If I could time it right then my fear of walking into crowded rooms would not trigger and send me into a hot flush. I would do this every day for four years.

Trust me; wherever you are now, I've been there and a lot worse.

When I was twenty eight, I decided to do something about the above! I started reading every book on confidence, NLP and pick up I could get my hands on. I watched DVD's and attended seminars. But things only finally changed two years after that, when I took action on what I'd learned and got out there.

I was sitting in Starbucks in Leeds in the north of England. I was going through a huge self-improvement process at the time; I was learning Italian from my book and then the phone rang. The guy introduced himself but it didn't click with me who I was talking to. A week before I had sent an email to a famous pick up company based in London with my suggestions for a video training they should do. Well evidently the CEO of the company had read the email and had one of his trainers phone me. Only the day before had I finished reading this trainers book. After twenty minutes of speaking to him, it clicked with me that I was talking to a guy called Dhurum who was based in London. In the prior weeks I had spent time watching Youtube videos of Dhurum picking up girls in central London. At the time I really liked his style of direct approach which resonated with me.

We arranged to meet up in Leicester Square a couple of weeks later. I handed over an envelope full of money and he introduced me to his wingman. Over the next two days, myself and the wingman walked around London randomly looking for girls to speak to. He would point the girls out and I would simply walk up to them and make my direct approaches. In two days I came away with around twenty phone numbers. I even had an "instant date" with a model which took up a large part of the day, preventing me from getting even more phone numbers. I was amazed at how easy I was finding doing what I had been fearing for so long.

I returned to Leeds knowing my life was changed. And it had!

I now knew I was one of the few guys who had the guts to walk up to nearly any woman, no matter who she was with or where she was or what she was doing and start a conversation with her. I had the ability to take that woman from the spot we met to the nearest Starbucks within only a few minutes.

While this book is not about picking up women, although that of course will be one of your goals, I am under no allusion as to that, picking up women with much ease will be a side effect of what you will learn in this book. For what happened next is most extraordinary.

Aged thirty three, I'm sitting in a bar in Oxford reading a book. Two women come and approach me while I'm minding my own business. This now happens regularly. Aged thirty three, women will make excuses to talk to me in everyday situations even when it makes no sense whatsoever. For example, they ask if they can borrow the seat next to me in an empty Starbucks, where there are many empty seats around. They ask me opinion openers in the supermarket (if you live in the UK you'll know it's almost taboo to speak to strangers). I've even seen girls at the gym follow me into exercise classes and return the week afterwards to see if I'm there. I often get women of all ages getting their friends to come over to me to see if I'm interested in their friend, who normally just happens to be watching us from a distance.

Why?

My looks have faded now I'm in my mid-thirties! So it must be something else.

In this book you're going to discover those alpha male traits and qualities that women are genetically programmed to sniff out. They can't help it. It's evolution, it's hard wired into their DNA.

This is not a traditional "pick up" book. I've already written one of those based on my experiences in London, from what I know works very well. This is not a book to help you with your approach anxiety; I have already written one of those based on a life of shyness to somebody who can approach despite that shyness. This book is about making you the very best person you can possibly be. It's about making you confident and attractive to women on the inside so that they'll be able to sense you are one of the 1% that all women crave.

Alpha Males – An Evolutionary Look

In the animal kingdom, the traditional example used when talking about alpha males is the lion. With all those dangerous lions around, fighting over the same food and the same females, the lion who gets the pick as well as his own way is the one who can stand his ground and fight off all other challenges from his male competitors.

However, this one lion, the alpha has responsibilities. It is up to the alpha to fend off predators that are a danger to the pride, especially to the younger cubs. As reward, the alpha gets the first choice when it comes to food and in selecting a female. The alpha is the only lion that is guaranteed to pass his lineage down to the next generation, ensuring the survival of the species. Being the strongest lion there, that is his reward.

As a consequence to being the alpha, he must endure constant challenges to his authority from the other male lions who correctly feel the urge to pass their genes down to the next generation. When he can fend off these challenges, by fighting them and defeating them, he guarantees he remains the alpha. However when a new challenger defeats him, this new upstart then becomes the new alpha and it is his genetics that are guaranteed to be passed down to the new generation of cubs. In fact it has even been observed that these new alpha lions then kill the cubs of the former alpha since female lions are unable to mate while they have cubs to look after.

All those lesser lions that are unable to match up to the alpha male are extremely unlikely to find a mate, procreate and pass down their genetic lineage to the next generation.

This is nature! It is brutal! It is unapologetic! It is survival of the fittest!

But there are many examples in the animal kingdom of how it's the dominant male who gets to have some alone time with the female, while all the lesser males remain outside in the cold, as prey for other animals. However, how male "dominance" is perceived differs widely from animal to animal, just as it does between lions and humans, thankfully.

The guppy fish has a very interesting way of showing off their vigour, daring, physical fitness as well as dominance in order to impress females. When predator fish swim near a school of guppies, the alpha males are known to swim up close to the predator in order to inspect the threat. When the predator takes the bait and tries to catch them, the guppies can show off their prowess by swimming away quickly and proving to the school that there is a genuine threat nearby. Those alpha male pretenders, who can't swim fast enough, will doubtless be eaten by the predator. Interestingly, it has been found that when all females are removed from the school, no male bothers trying to be alpha by swimming up close to the danger. Under laboratory conditions, it has indeed been found that females prefer these more daring of males over the other guppies. It's not hard to reason that these guppies that swim up close and can easily escape from the predator would be more physically fit than the other guppies. What fish does not want to pass physical fitness down to the next generation?

In a study of barn swallows, it was found that females will actively seek out those males with longer tail feathers. It was discovered that males with longer tail feathers had fewer parasitical blood-sucking mites that cause disease and infection. Since these mites jump from swallow to swallow, those with longer tails were better able to keep those parasites at a safe distance. Over time this will of course result in more swallow chicks with long tails being born, while their shorter tailed brothers will be bred out of existence. My point being however, that of course, in many species, females actively seek out males who exhibit certain traits. In this case females are seeking out those healthy males who will be able to sire healthy offspring.

In the wild, budgies are known to single out from birth, those chicks with different coloured feathers and kick them out from the nest. "Birds of a feather, fly together" is a saying that is extremely true as those chicks who look different from the rest of their flock are less likely to find a mate. Doubtless these different looking chicks will be eaten by predators on the ground. Female budgies have been found to strongly prefer those males with brighter green and yellow feathers, probably because stronger colours stimulate the senses more. Why is this important?

Well it's probably because those males with brighter feathers are easier to find, they stand out more in the trees. If they are easier to find then the female spends less time searching, thus being exposed to predators. It's about security!

Now let's introduce the concept of social proof by taking a quick look at the grouse. It has been observed that certain males will receive up to 80% of all female attention while breeding. It was also discovered that females will gravitate towards the formerly lesser popular males when researchers placed stuffed female grouse dummies in their proximity.

So why do female grouse select these males with other females around them when they could quite easily go for those males with less competition? As you'll discover later on, social proof is of paramount importance. In the case of the grouse, if a certain male appears to have an abundance of females around him, it proves he is pre-selected. He must therefore be more attractive, stronger and more able to sire healthier chicks than the male grouse with no females around him. In essence, it is a time saving device. The female does not need to waste time discovering if these qualities exist in all the other males, if all the other females have together already carried out the work and found a male with what they desire.

Returning to our guppy friends and those daring males who swim close to their predators, it was also found that the alpha fish, as well as being faster swimmers, also had more orange colours. As well as swimming ability, it would appear that females also tend to prefer more orange males too. Not picky at all are they! However, it was found that this desire for orange was overridden when other females had already chosen a less orange male. This is social proof in action, in the fish world. When the paired males only differed slightly, up to around 25%, it was always the male already with a female that was the most desirable. When this threshold changed however and the differences in orange increased to 40%, then the females would return to the more orange guppies regardless of what the other females were doing.

This probably goes to show that social proof is extremely important, up to an extent. After all, if you surround a tramp with beautiful women, are other women necessarily expected to find the tramp attractive? Common sense would say no! However, if the tramp was to scrub up, buy some new clothes, surround himself with women and read this book, then he could certainly do very well.

Let's now leave the animal kingdom and take a closer look at what women are looking for in men. What are those alpha male traits that the female of our species is genetically programmed to search for.

Part 2

Alpha Male Elements

Alpha Male Traits and Characteristics

Why do animals have all these very strange traits and behaviours in order to attract a mate? Bright feathers, long feathers, fast swimming, fighting ability and we barely even scratched the surface with animals. They are displays to show they are strong, healthy, capable food gatherers and will be able to provide for their young. It is about convincing the female that they will make the best possible father for the next generation.

So what are the traits that humans go for? What are those alpha male characteristics that women look for in men in order prove that they too will make excellent choices as fathers.

We humans have progressed beyond simply fighting with our peers to attract a female. However as you'll see, we may not actually be all that different from many animals.

This book is about becoming the best possible guy you can be. Women can sense when a guy is in the top 5% of desirable males or higher. To become that guy, it's not about memorising lines and routines, magic tricks or stories. It's more about becoming the best possible version of yourself you can possibly become so that when women see you, they just know. I can't explain how they know it when they see you, but they just do! After all, can't you sense a lot of things about women when you see them?

Now I'm going to be honest here and say that it's not possible to become this guy overnight. It probably won't even happen in the near future. I'm not even properly there myself yet, in fact I have a long way still to go to be where I want to be. It's an on-going process, a constant battle to improve yourself, always pushing yourself to become even better and that is how you should see it. Don't forget that there are always other guys out there learning new skills and becoming more desirable to the opposite sex. So you must take the mind-set that if you yourself are not always progressing then you are not simply staying stagnant, but you are in fact going backwards. If you are not in a constant battle to improve yourself, for yourself and not for anybody else, then other guys will overtake you.

The following section will make up a large part of this book. Some of the elements you'll be able to put in place almost immediately. However, the vast majority of what I'm going to be suggesting to you to become that most desirable of men, the alpha male, will be an on-going process to personal fulfilment.

Here are the alpha male elements which we'll go into in detail:

- Physical Attraction
- Confidence
- Ambition
- Displays of Expertise
- Social Proof
- Leadership
- Ability to Connect
- Life Experience

Alpha Element # 1

Physical Attraction

By buying this book, you have made a commitment to better yourself. And I'm sure also that you'd prefer I give you it straight up and not try and sugar coat my opinions. After all, alpha males speak their mind, right!

Yes, looks do matter!

They certainly are not the be-all-and-end-all but being reasonably attractive will certainly do yourself no harm when it comes to being an alpha male, attracting the opposite sex and indeed, having them make the approaches to *you*. Don't we guys put a heck of a lot of importance on looks when it comes to women? Well, I can promise you that they do as well, although thankfully, not as much importance as we guys do and not as much importance as they put on other factors that you'll discover later on.

But obviously, we're aiming for the full package here and so being physically attractive is a very important part of all that. Remember that women are programmed to seek out males that have good genes to pass down to the next generation. They will instinctively know that passing down attractive genes will do their kids a lot of good.

It may be that you are already a physically attractive person, in which case good luck with that. All I know is that having reasonably good looks did not do me any favours whatsoever once I was actually around girls in my teenage years. They will be worthless if you have to rely on them. But if you have them as well as the rest of the package, then you will certainly be in the very top percentage of alpha males.

Besides, if there is something unsightly about you or if you've never spent any real time in the gym, then this will quite possibly be the source of much insecurity about yourself. Alpha males are not insecure! Alpha males instead think, sorry, *know* they are the shit!

So think about those elements of your physical appearance you could improve and write them down. We all have them. They could be very obscure things as well, for example, I used to have an extremely runny nose. I used to have to blow my nose every few minutes. Imagine being around somebody that has to do that, and naturally it made me very paranoid about what people were thinking about me. So what did I do? I dealt with it! I had an operation on my nose to stop the transparent fluid from streaming down every few minutes. Immediately afterwards, that whole barrier from my life was removed. It made me feel a lot better about myself not having to blow my nose in front of everybody every few minutes.

Over the last ten years I've worked on a tonne of things I wasn't happy about. Each little thing took me that bit closer to where I wanted to be. I'm not talking about plastic surgery, that is completely unnecessary but there are many things you can do to improve your appearance. You need to think what it is you're unhappy about and then do something about each one of them. Below are the most common things you can improve:

Style

It was Shakespeare who said "The clothes maketh the man!" And this is very true!

As an experiment, I have walked around my local city looking my very best except from the clothes I was wearing, just to gather the interest I got from the girls. I groomed myself up to the max and styled my hair. However, I dressed in faded blue jeans, a hoody and trainers. I walked around trying to make eye contact with girls and, not surprisingly I didn't get very much interest.

Later on that week, I decided not to shower or shave and I didn't style my hair either. I did however dress in my finest casual clothes consisting of extremely well-fitting and expensive jeans, shirt and stylish overcoat with shoes. The difference was quite eye opening. You will get a lot more attention from girls by dressing well. It's all about your style.

Style is everything!

I'm no expert on style, though I do know what looks good on me. I used to spend quite a bit of money on expensive clothes and I still got only a few positive reactions from them. That was until I decided to have a closer look at what the most important elements of clothing were.

In my opinion, one of the most important things you can do with regards to your clothes is to have an extremely good fit. You really do not want to have anything, your jeans, pants or shirts being oversized and baggy. When you next go to the store, you need to try on a few different sizes to get the very best tight fit. Ever since I discovered that, I can shop at any old clothes store, buy budget clothes and still look and feel awesome. It's all about the fit.

As for what you actually wear, that will depend on what looks good on you, everybody is different. Why not take a look at a few men's magazines, or better yet, open your eyes when you're out and about and take a good look at what other stylish men are wearing. Find a style that you like the look of and replicate it for yourself, adding in your own little twists and quirks.

A good rule of thumb is to aim for two different colours, or no more than three. It is of paramount importance that the colour of your shoes matches the colour of your belt. Brown shoes plus belt will go great with any jeans with a blue shade. Black will go with most colours.

You should also look into accessories. Smart shoulder man bags are all the rage these days, so I highly suggest you take a look at a few different styles. If you live in a cold city then a stylish scarf is also a really cool accessory to have. If your accessories match the colour of your shoes and belt then that will be a great advantage.

Just find a style that suits you and makes you feel alive. Having a good sense of style will more than make up for any deficiencies in the looks department. I highly recommend you invest some extensive time in this area.

Body

Naturally, alpha males need to have a strong and healthy body, which again is more important than having a photogenic face.

Many women put muscles quite high up on their agenda, so if you're not already a member of a gym then you should consider signing up for one. I suggest you look for a large gym that also has classes running throughout the day. Classes are great places for meeting women, in fact they are one of the places I've been known to do quite well at.

If you are overweight, or feel you could lose just a little bit of fat, then by far the best method of training is HIIT. HIIT stands for High Intensity Interval Training and there is a book by James Driver on that very subject that will quite possibly change your life.

Why does HIIT work so well? It is because it is intensive! When most people go for a run, they do so at an intensity of around 70% for an average of 45 minutes. Coming from an evolutionary perspective, no animal ever evolved due to stress at 70%! It takes a lot more than that. HIIT involves short bursts of all out sprints at 100% of your maximum intensity, followed by periods of walking. The walks are easy and makes the all-out sprints tolerable and even fun. But because you are giving your body more stress, the body makes much greater and much faster changes and it will do so in only a fraction of the time of a normal 45 minute jogging session.

Seriously, if you take any of my advice from this book, you need to invest in HIIT by James Driver.

Yes, HIIT will take care of any excess body fat you have and it will do so quickly and in a fun way. But you should also work on building up your general strength by doing weights too. Not only will strength training build up your muscles, it will also improve your posture and overall confidence. You get so many benefits from working out, that I'm sure you're already aware of that it truly is worth putting in an hour, three times a week.

Complexion

This was a major one for me as I was growing up. As soon as I hit 17 the spots and acne decided they were going to turn my life into a complete misery and they persisted for several years. If you are affected by this then I know it can ruin your life if you allow it. I was on internship wages at the time (£35 per week) and at least half of that money would go on creams, lotions, witch hazel sticks, ointments and prescribed remedies to treat my skin. I even once tried a homemade recipe which I remember contained paprika. I would smear this paprika paste all over my face before I went to bed. I would arrive at work the next day and people would ask why my face was stained orange. I even once went a full month washing my face once every hour to clean away the sebum; that just gave me a rash. I tried lots of things to try and improve my skin and get my confidence back.

One thing I noticed about all these "cures" is that many of them actually worked, at least for a short period before my skin became used to the treatment and would then become immune to it. This could happen in as short a period of time as two weeks; your skin becoming resistant to the treatments. You can now have special therapy that can clear up extreme cases but thankfully my condition improved before this was necessary.

One day I simply became completely fed up with spending the majority of my meagre wages on all these products that I just stopped, threw them all away and decided I was going to leave it to god. At the same time I started to drink a lot of water which is the main reason my complexion improved.

- Contrary to some beliefs, spots and acne have nothing to do with your diet or environment. It is completely down to genetics and most people are affected by this in their lives.
- Do not buy any product that aims to improve your complexion, they do not work and are a waste of money.
- Drink plenty of water. Aim for 6 litres a day, ideally you should always have your bottle of water on you. Take a short gulp once every 5 minutes. This is free and will have other health benefits for your body. Within a few weeks your complexion will improve dramatically and if you can stay in the habit of drinking water like I have, the effects will be permanent.

Seriously guys, if you have a bad complexion, water will do more good for you than anything else. The key is to take small amounts extremely often. You will be surprised at how quickly things will improve for you.

Teeth

How many times have you seen an attractive girl only to see her teeth are not all that great? Wouldn't you agree that this is probably the one physical imperfection that would make the most difference to a person's looks? Girls are a lot less fussy about looks on men than we are with women. The exception to this rule though is with the teeth. I cannot emphasise enough to you the importance of having nice, straight white teeth. Don't believe me? Then ask any of your female friends how important nice teeth on guys are.

Teeth are one of the signs of a person's overall health, if your teeth are unhealthy, then so probably is the person they belong to. I really do hope that this section is something you won't have to spend much time and effort on (again, ask yourself honestly) in which case you should skip it. Ideally you should have had frequent trips to the dentist throughout your childhood and you should have great teeth.

If you have any missing teeth, overlapping, gaps or discolourment in there then you really should get them fixed. The vast majority of people shouldn't have any problems here but I personally know 3 people who have had complete replacement surgery carried out and it has improved their quality of life dramatically. If you are in the UK or the US then this can be very expensive. You can go to places like Hungary or Argentina to have this surgery carried out at a massively reduced price and have a holiday at the same time.

If your teeth are merely a little stained, as general life will make that happen then you can visit a dental hygienist who can truly effectively clean them up. You will be amazed at the difference a single trip to the dentist can make for the colour of your teeth. From then on you only need yearly maintenance visits to keep them pearly white on a permanent basis.

Hair

I know from experience that having a decent hair style makes a big difference. Girls love it when a guy has nice hair because they like to run their hands through it, much like we guys like doing to women in fact.

Note then differences in attention you get from women when you're out and about when you put a little bit of effort into having a nice hair style. Trust me, it makes a big difference.

Again, I am no hair expert, but I know what looks good on me. This is because once a year I go to an expensive salon and ask to have their advice on what would look best on me. They take into account how much hair you actually have, colour and the shape of your face and they'll give you something that will make you look attractive. Then all you simply need to do is photograph it and the next time you go for a haircut, at any old inexpensive place, all you need to do is show the stylist your photo. This way you can have the same classy hairstyle but for a fraction of the price.

Try it! It'll be worth it and will make a big difference.

Summary

You may have read books that tell you looks don't matter, but trust me they do! Once again, looks are not everything, but they are certainly a very large piece of the overall alpha male puzzle.

If you're going to be making a commitment to yourself to embark on a self-improvement journey then it would be foolish not to take into account all elements, and of course this includes your looks.

When you consider all the other areas in this book to become an alpha male, it is in fact the looks and physical attractiveness aspects that will be the easiest for many people. Depending on your starting point, this category will take the least amount of time when compared to much of the remaining advice in this book.

In most cases, what it will require is perhaps a small amount of financial investment. But in the case of fixing your teeth this will be a one off financial investment that will benefit you for the rest of your life.

By picking that one part of yourself that is and has always been causing your discomfort and eliminating it, not only are you improving your looks, you are also improving your confidence by default. Which brings us to our next section.

Alpha Element # 2

Confidence

It will come as no shock to you that confidence is all important. Often, it is that very confidence that personifies the alpha male. I could write a full book on confidence. In fact, I already did!

Confidence is something that you will undoubtedly develop over time. Like I said, becoming an alpha male is not something you can do overnight.

For confidence to develop, you first need to become competent!

Let me explain that a little.

Think of something you're really good at? Perhaps you go to yoga classes every week and have been doing so for a few years now. Are you confident when it comes to yoga? Yes you will be and that is because you are competent at yoga. You will know all about the many yoga poses, postures, holds and stretches so that if anybody who is just starting out at yoga comes and asks you how to do it, you'd be able to give them detailed explanations and demonstrations to help them get good too.

Imagine if you moved town and so went to a different yoga class and all the people there were new faces. If you met these new people at a dance class and not a yoga class, you'd probably be really nervous. But because you're meeting them for the first time while doing something you're comfortable and well-practiced at, it'll be a piece of cake.

In fact if you're looking to meet women, classes are really good places to start particularly if you're already really good at that activity. This is because you will already feel confident within that venue. Women will be able to see that too because you will be standing out from the crowd.

I was a break dancer for ten years. That was my thing and I got very good at being able to do all those really cool and crazy moves you see in the dance videos. I used to attend classes all over the country with people I'd never met before and even though I was far from an alpha male back then, or even very confident in every day settings, I still stood out from the rest of the break dancers. This was because I was good at it, which made me confident within the room. People would come and ask for my advice on pulling off certain moves. They would see me do a windmill, pretzel or a spinning worm whilst lying on my back and they would approach me and ask for me to teach it to them too. If I was in the company of break dancers anywhere in the country, then I was confident. However, if you were to plonk me in the middle of a street dance class, or even a yoga class then I'd certainly be the guy asking whoever looked confident for help.

Competence = Confidence!

In the context of wanting to become confident with women, then yes you are going to have to become competent with that first. Which of course means first having to spend time getting things wrong. But having confidence, or at least being able to fake it until you make it will help you out in abundance.

Let's take a look at some strategies to help you at least appear confident on the outside.

Body Language

Out of everything in this book, having confident and relaxed looking body language is perhaps the easiest and quickest thing to master in order to raise you up a few rungs on the alpha male hierarchy. Whole books have been written about body language, it really is a huge area. Through body language, you are more able to show your confidence than through all other forms of communication put together. It really is crucial to becoming a more confident person, or at least being perceived by others as well as feeling it yourself that you master confident body language.

In fact this is a clear example of life imitating art. When looking around certain rooms, you can sense who appears confident through their body language. Usually those confident looking guys are the ones who appear most relaxed. But how do you know they are actually really confident people? They could have read this book and done everything I said in order to look confident, even though they may not be. But the truth is that you can alter people's behaviour (confidence) on a temporary basis simply by modifying their positioning (body language).

You can easily tell a confident person just by looking at their body language. But did you know it's even possible to become more confident and more open simply by using body language to your advantage?

When you're speaking to people while your arms are crossed, you will naturally be more defensive. However, if you actually drop your arms by your sides, you will actually feel yourself becoming more open and friendly. This works incredibly well! Likewise, you can also open up the front of your arms to people to create a similar effect.

I'll let you into a little secret. I used to be a dating coach a few years back before I took to writing informative guides for men such as this one. I used to teach a very powerful technique to the guys to help get women to open up to them and start being more friendly. I taught my clients that while they were on a date with a girl or if they were chatting to a girl in a bar and she had her arms folded then they could simply unfold them by complementing the girl on something and then giving them a high five. The girls arms almost never returned to the folded position and the girl would always open up and become friendlier. There have been many studies published that confirm this and more, that our body language actually commands how we feel in the moment and can therefore alter our state confidence.

I hope I've demonstrated that while yes, confident people will use more active body language, but it's equally true that by using active body language, you'll feel more confident as well. This is what I mean by life imitating art.

I recommend that you watch TV presenters and actors and mimic how they use body language. Try and gauge the correct amount to use, as it actually can be quite easy to overdo it if you're not careful. If in doubt, practice in the mirror.

So let's have a look at some examples of positive body language which you should be using:

1. Hand Gestures – You can easily practice your hand gestures in the mirror. This really is simple to do yet easy to overdo so try and strike up a balance. Simply bend your arms at the elbow when you speak and make slow gestures with your hands. You can increase the movement and intensity when you make a point in order to emphasise it. If you do feel yourself becoming nervous while you speak, especially if you're making a speech in front of a large group of people, one thing you can do is steeple your hands. This shows power and confidence which will certainly mask any nerves. Watch how politicians steeple their hands; it's an indicator of who the leader is.

2. Take Up Space – Confident people aren't afraid to spread themselves out a little. Next time you're in a meeting, spread your papers out around the table, move your coffee cup to the edge of your personal area. When you're sitting down, spread your legs out a little bit. Don't be afraid to prop your arm over the head of the chair next to you. This shows dominance and confidence. Think about how you lounge about the house when you're at home on the sofa and there's nothing there to alter your state. You feel relaxed, which is why you look relaxed and vice versa. Try and imitate this to a degree when you're

out, at work or in a bar. When standing up, spread your feet out a little more to take up more of the floor area. This will give your body as well as your mind a "firmer footing."

3. Keep Your Movements Slow – Always be slow and controlled. Confident people are the exact opposite of erratic. Everything they do is calm, slow and deliberate. This shows you're in control of your body and there is nothing out there that can intimidate you. This should also include your hand gestures as described above, which should also be slow and comfortable.

4. Lower Your Drink – The majority of people keep their drinks close to their chest at all times. Similar to having folded arms, this acts as a barrier between you and everybody else. We do this for protection because we are nervous or uncomfortable. Always lower your drink and keep it by your side. Confident people are open and don't need a wall between themselves and the people they are in the same room as.

5. Hand Shaking – When you shake someone's hand, do so with a good firm grip to show you're a real man and not a wet blanket. Another thing you can do to show your confidence is to give them a pat on the shoulder with your free hand. This is a subtle way of saying "I'm in charge here!" Just be careful you don't do this at a job interview. Notice how politicians and world leaders especially always pat each other on the back when they're instructing one another, leading them around etc. As a general rule of

thumb, the guy who gives the final pat on the back to the other guy is the guy in charge. Did you see how Barack Obama and Mit Romney were patting each other hard and repeatedly on their backs during the presidential debating events? Finally, there was an extremely famous occasion in the Middle East where two politicians refused to walk through the door first because they each wanted to pat the other guy on the back as he walked through. Not to mention that neither wanted to be patted on the back by the other guy in front of the TV cameras.

Use with caution to show your alpha dominance over the other guy, but just as importantly, realise when others are doing it to you.

Now let's take a look at some negative body language traits you should try and cut out:

1. Fidgeting – This is a big one and something all of us do unconsciously. We fidget mainly because we're nervous. Nervousness just happens to be the exact opposite of confidence so I suggest you try and consciously cut nervous traits out of your being. Simply by incorporating the positive body language traits above into yourself, you'll feel more confident anyway and fidgeting should automatically be reduced on its own. However, if you have any nervous ticks or you tap your fingers or feet then you must try and stop this. Do you often play with your cell phone just to give your hands something to do? This is fidgeting! Do you often take small sips of your drink for similar reasons? Try and cut this out. Do you touch your

face or cover your mouth when speaking. This shows nervousness in a big way and that you don't actually believe what it is you're actually saying. Liars cover their mouth when they speak without even realising it.

2. Don't Cross Your Arms – We've already covered this! By folding your arms you are creating a wall between yourself and everybody else. This shows insecurity and discomfort. On top of that, it actually makes your whole attitude feel closed and shut off. Try speaking to your friends with your arms folded and then feel the difference when you unfold them, thus opening your body up. It's funny how things work sometimes.

3. Don't look down – This goes for when standing, sitting or walking. Looking down at the floor conveys weakness; defeated people look down. By holding your head up, you are exposing your neck, which evolutionary speaking is an extremely weak area. Therefore you are showing dominance by looking up because you don't expect any predator to dare make an attack on your weak and unprotected spot. Notice how Superman always looks up. He knows nobody is going to attack him and for good reason.

4. Don't smile too much – We smile mainly because people have done something that we like and that we want to show our appreciation for what they have just said or done. We smile because we want to them to like us. While there's nothing wrong with this, there is a lot wrong with doing it too much because it shows you're trying too hard

to get them to like you. When in actual fact, you need to be thinking in the opposite direction. It's them who need to try to get you to like them. Excessive smiling not only shows neediness on your part but it will also come across as being false, especially to women who are used to having guys trying to get her to like them. Smile only when it's deserved. That way, it'll mean an awful lot more when you do smile.

5. Don't react too quickly – Alpha males are supposed to be calm. Nothing gets them worked up, hot and bothered. If somebody calls to you then don't snap your head looking around for who it was. Be slow, calm and controlled. Whenever there's panic in a room, notice how people always look towards the guy who's sat there unreactive; the calm person. Rather coincidentally, this usually happens to be the alpha male.

Posture

It should come as no surprise to you that our posture is an integral part of how we look and how others perceive us.

For many of us, having great posture is something we don't need to think about because we have it naturally anyway. However, for most of us, we need to be making a conscious effort to be upright when out and about.

In fact, scientific studies have now proven the link between our postures and our confidence and self-belief.

It has been proved that when we sit up straight, with great postures, we have more belief in what it is we're saying.

Seventy-one Ohio State University students took part in a study, the purpose of which was kept from them. Instead, they were told they were taking part in two different studies, one to do with acting (holding various poses while doing other things), and one about business and job performance. They were asked to write down their best or worst qualities while they were sitting down with their back erect and pushing their chest out (confident posture) or slouched forward with their back curved (doubtful posture). Then, they completed a number of questions and reported their self-evaluations. These included evaluating whether they thought they were qualified or able to do certain jobs.

Confidence in what the students had said, good or bad, was significantly greater when students wrote their thoughts in the confident than in the doubtful posture. The students did not especially feel more confident in the "confident posture," but they did believe the things they had written more when they were in that posture instead of the "doubtful posture."

That means we are not even aware of our posture's influence on our confidence in what we say or write! Our posture directly affects how much we believe what we're communicating, and it's not just a matter of tricking ourselves by squaring our shoulders and "feeling confident."

In fact, the results were striking! How the students rated themselves as future professionals depended on which posture they held as they wrote the positive or negative traits. Students who held the upright, confident posture were much more likely to rate themselves in line with the positive or negative traits they wrote down. In other words, if they wrote positive traits about themselves, they rated themselves more highly, and if they wrote negative traits about themselves, they rated themselves lower.

However, students who assumed the slumped over, less confident posture didn't seem convinced by their own thoughts – their ratings didn't differ much regardless of whether they wrote positive or negative things about themselves.

The author of the study says, "Most of us were taught that sitting up straight gives a good impression to other people, but it turns out that our posture can also affect how we think about ourselves. If you sit up straight, you end up convincing yourself by the posture you're in."

So you can see the clear benefits to our confidence in maintaining a good posture at all times. This is something we all need to be working on.

So how can you improve your posture? Well there are a few techniques you can use such as these below:

1. The balloon technique – While walking or standing, imagine there's a balloon on a string extending from the crown of your head. Imagine the balloon is pulling your head upwards towards the sky. This will automatically make you stand upright with your spine elongated.

2. Keep in alignment – Try and keep your ears, shoulders and hips in perfect alignment when sitting. This will force you to sit up straight.

3. Pull in your abs when walking. This is perhaps the part where you're making the most effort, but also getting the most return too.

4. When sitting, keep the soles of your feet flat on the floor.

5. Be consistent – This means making a conscious effort to have great posture all the time. I know this can be a pain, but before long it will become natural.

Eye Contact

I almost didn't include this part because it really is very obvious, but I suppose no book on being an alpha male would be complete without a mention on eye contact, so here goes.

Have you ever spoken to somebody who isn't looking at you while you speak to them? There are usually two reasons why they choose to do this. Either they are nervous speaking to you and so look away out of intimidation. Or they are so alpha that they don't feel the need to look you in the eyes when *you're* speaking. Powerful people are not afraid to look into the eyes of the person they're speaking to, they are also not afraid to look away and do their own thing while people are talking to them. However, when alphas speak themselves, they almost always look the other guy in the eye and command their attention.

If you're in conversation with somebody and you're uncomfortable with prolonged eye contact then there's nothing wrong with breaking it for a few seconds or longer, in fact this is something I recommend. If you're listening to somebody speak, you can break eye contact to take a sip of your drink, check your watch or phone. Otherwise feel free to stare straight ahead, or even to glaze over when you're listening to others. You can even look down and carry on with what you were doing; just try not to come over as rude. Guys, this does not go for job interviews or when being introduced to a girl's parents.

Remember that when it is you speaking, you really should be looking the other person in the eye. This is because what you have to say is important and you need to be commanding the other person's full attention.

Facial Expressions

It is said that when we speak to people, the words we actually say account only for 10% of the overall message. While body language accounts for well over half, the exact number is debated.

There are two main aspects to body language. Firstly there is your actual body language and secondly there are your facial expressions.

If you're curious what makes up the rest of the pie while we're speaking, it's a mixture of smiling and eye contact which we've already covered, voice tonality which we will cover in a bit and how you're actually speaking which we'll also cover.

The next time you're speaking to the people around you, take note of their actual facial expressions. What do you notice? I'm guessing you'll notice that not many people's facial expressions actually change while they talk. Most of us tend to keep a normal and straight face while we're talking to people. What message does this put across? Well it says you're not very interested in the conversation for one, but it also shows a lack of confidence.

The next time you're watching TV, take note of newsmen and TV presenters and watch their facial expressions while they speak. These people are the masters of the facial expression. They have to be! They got the job because they're able to draw people in primarily with their faces.

Watch a movie tonight and watch the actors and how they use facial expressions to convey passion, interest, humour and a whole host of other emotions.

This is just one of the reasons why people on TV always come over as being super confident.

You need to get into the habit of showing your emotion and interest in people when you speak to them by using expressive facial signals. In all honesty, not many people do this out in the real world and by being one of the few who does, you'll stand out for sure.

Practice talking in the mirror, don't laugh, I mean it, it'll be a great exercise for you. You need to get the balance right so that you don't look like you're overdoing it but instead it should come over as being completely natural.

This is so easy to do and it'll make such a huge difference to how confident and alpha you're perceived by others.

Voice Speed and Tonality

The speed and tonality in which we speak together make up the rest of how we are perceived by others while communicating. The speed you speak at and your tone of voice together are actually a lot more important to showing how confident you are than what it is you're actually saying.

Once again, I'm going to ask you to pay close attention to TV presenters and news anchors to learn from the masters.

Voice tonality in particular can be used to great effect. By alternating your pitch you will come over as being extremely interesting simply because practically nobody does it. You can use voice tonality to emphasise points and a lot more on top of that. The best way to describe how you should aim to sound is by saying you should talk with emotion. If you'd like to hear a great motivational speaker who can draw you in through voice tonality then watch a few Youtube videos featuring Tony Robbins.

With regards to speed, I'll say you should speak in a slow, calm and controlled way. By speaking slowly, you're showing your dominance and confidence. Have you ever spoken to somebody who speaks really quickly? This always makes them come over as being nervous and even erratic which clearly is not good.

In general you should always try and speak slowly and calmly however I'll also say that in order to sound a little more interesting, there's nothing wrong with alternating your speed a little bit just like you should be alternating your pitch. However, don't overdo this and use your best judgement. Think Brad Pitt in Fight Club!

I was advising one of my friends on voice speed. He is one of those who stops people in the street to sign them up to a charity. His problem was that people kept on walking away from him when he spoke, a big problem for many of these street charity people. When I saw him in the street working, I told him his problem was that he was speaking too quickly and he'd have more success if he slowed down a little. Because he spoke really quickly, he gave off the impression that what he had to say was not important and that speaking fast helped to get his message over before people had the chance to run. He confirmed to me that this was why he spoke quickly. When I told him to slow the speed he was speaking at he told me he was afraid people would get bored of him and the end effect would still be the same. I made him realise that those thoughts were killing his confidence. Together we practiced his message in a more slow and controlled way. The results? Over the next week he had an increase of around 50% in signups.

Why was the increase so dramatic? Because by speaking slower, you are demonstrating complete confidence and belief in what you're saying.

As I mentioned earlier, if you adopt these confidence strategies into your being, you will actually feel real confidence within yourself. This will then further perpetuate more confidence from you. It's a positive spiral that all begins by learning all the above methods that help you appear confident on the outside, that will of course make you feel confidence on the inside.

All the above confidence strategies are of course body language techniques that combined will really change your life. Now let's take a look at some different strategies that are more intervention based. These strategies are designed to build up your confidence by pushing your boundaries that little bit further.

"The only way to expand your comfort zone is to live outside it!"

Charlie Valentino

Expose Yourself

I don't mean that literally. By exposing yourself I mean you should be doing little things every day that makes you uncomfortable.

When we try to build our muscles, we have to stress them as much as possible. Well to build our confidence we need to stress our minds.

All you really need to do is quit playing everything so safe. When you go to the coffee shop, don't automatically sit with your back to the wall, but instead sit in the middle of the room where everybody can see you. When you next go to a bar do likewise.

Next time you're standing in line, open up a conversation with some random stranger. Practically nobody does this as it's seen as taboo to speak to strangers, so you'll stand out a lot.

Next time you're at college or university, sit at the front where the lecturers typically pick on you. Volunteer to answer questions or to express an opinion in front of everybody. If you don't do this regularly then you'll feel a change within yourself by speaking out in front of so many people and so often. You'll never have a better chance than at college to speak out and push yourself so much. You really should take full advantage.

Why not take things to the next level and volunteer to do some sort of public speaking at university? One of my friends, who was already very confident by the way, volunteered to show a crowd of prospective students around the campus giving a talk along the way.

The same techniques for body language still apply when you're speaking in front of large groups. In fact by applying those techniques and by speaking with passion you'll have their full attention. Try alternating your eye contact between everybody watching you. It'll give you quite a thrill.

If you're not a student then volunteer to speak out at work or in the office. If you don't have a job that has this kind of potential for you then you should look online for a local improvisation class. Basically improv is acting on the spot, on your feet and in front of a group of people. You will be given a subject to act out with a group and you will play a role within that group. There are few things in existence that will build up your confidence better than an improve class.

All these little things add up, plus you never know who you'll meet along the way.

Disagree with People

Disagreeing with the people around you is one of life's great pleasures, and that is how you should see it.

Nobody likes people who simply agree with them on everything they say simply because they think it'll make them more popular. Attractive women in particular are used to men agreeing with them on everything and it really does not come over as being sincere, attractive and certainly not alpha.

One of the principle things that makes confident people stand out from the rest of the crowd is their ability to disagree with others. On the flip side, how is agreeing with people on everything, especially if you don't actually agree with it any way to live your life? What does that say about us if we agree with people even if we actually think the opposite?

You really should make the effort to disagree with your friends, family and peers whenever the opportunity arises. Just make sure it's sincere and you're not just doing it for the sake of it. You're not playing devil's advocate here; you're trying to be alpha male.

Feel free to disagree on the small things and the big things and everything in between.

However, it's important to realise the difference between disagreeing and having an argument. The two things are completely different and you should remember that.

Arguments can blow up out of all proportion which is not the desired effect you're trying to make, whereas a disagreement is something that is done constructively within the context of a conversation.

Do it and enjoy it!

This concludes our section on confidence. We will now move on to one trait that many women rate even higher than confidence.

Alpha Element # 3

Ambition

There are a great many women out there who list ambition as the number 1 quality they look for in a man. Ambition is an extremely attractive quality for us guys to have! There are many women out there who get into relationships with guys and then end it, citing lack of ambition as the reason for the break-up of the relationship. If the guy isn't going anywhere in his life, then she will reason that he will hold her back too. This is a shame but in many cases it's the truth.

Why not ask a few of your female friends if they think ambition is an important quality in a man. See what they say!

You should also ask them if they think they can sense if a man is ambitious simply by looking at him. The answers you get may surprise you.

Ask yourself if you are an ambitious man!

It is so very important that you are aspiring for better things down the line and that you are not simply settling for your present position, no matter what it may be.

You may be reading this and thinking that you are already happy and settled in your work or that you can't possibly go any higher in your field. For example, maybe you are already an airline pilot, or you already own your own company. In that case, what are you doing to try and improve life for all airline pilots? What are you doing to grow that company that you own?

In the vast majority of cases however, I'm going to go out on a limb and assume that most guys reading this book are not in fact working in their dream jobs with a six figure income.

Let me tell you now that it does not matter what you are doing right at this moment in time! It does not matter if you are a student, if you work in some lowly office position that you hate, if you are on an apprenticeship, it doesn't matter if you work on a check out and it certainly doesn't matter if you work at McDonalds. All that matters is that you have a desire to better your position and you *are actively doing something to change it.*

Remember, that if you're not growing, you're shrinking because other people around you, those people who are going after the same promotions as you, the same women as you, they are all growing.

You need to make sure you are growing at a faster pace than everybody else.

Let's take a few examples, and we'll make it difficult for ourselves by taking a few extreme examples to demonstrate my point.

Harry is 19, he has worked at McDonalds for two years. Harry loves working at McDonalds and when he speaks about it, people can see this in him. You see, the difference is that Harry has a plan. McDonalds are investing in Harry to go to chef school. Every day, Harry works flipping burgers and serving customers quarter pounder meals. But three nights a week, Harry goes to college to learn how to become a chef. In his spare time he experiments with his own recipes at home and he tests them out on his friends and family and gets their feedback. When his parents invite friends over to the house, Harry insists on doing all the cooking and testing out his new recipes that he created on the guests. Harry is compiling a book of these recipes, which are all English classics. Harry intends to sell this book online and he even hopes to have the book published. Harry also intends to open up his own restaurant, he just needs to finish chef school first so that then he can quit McDonalds and dedicate all his time to his dream.

Suddenly, working at McDonalds doesn't sound so bad does it! Do you think there would be many girls that Harry talks to who would be put off by the fact he works at McDonalds after hearing the rest of his story?

Kieron works on the checkout at the local supermarket. He hates it but everybody has to work. What he really wants to do is to become an artist. He knows it's hard to get into, selling your own paintings for a living. He knows also that there are not many opportunities around for being a full time artist. So Kieron puts up with working on the checkout for the time being. However, on his days off, he volunteers at the local art gallery. This enables him to work within his chosen industry and gain valuable experience. He also gets to meet and learn from other people and other artists who are already doing what he wants to do. He is making contacts and connections. In his spare time he paints his pictures, expanding his portfolio. He has created a website for himself where he showcases his work and tries to make a name for himself. He attends as many art shows as he can get to and he is always trying to learn more and improve himself within his craft. Becoming a full time artist is very tough. But Kieron has a plan and every day he knows he is getting one step closer to achieving his dream.

What do Harry and Kieron both have in common? They both work in jobs that would put many women off wanting to get to know them better. But they both have a plan! An action plan that they are actively working with to improve their situations. Every day, they are getting just that little bit closer to achieving their dreams.

Ambition is an incredible quality to have! But actually having a plan and actually executing a little piece of that plan every single day is putting that ambition into practice. That is what makes all the difference.

Let's now take a look at Andy.

Andy is in his mid-thirties and had worked for a construction company for fifteen years before the company hit hard times and made Andy and several of his colleagues redundant. Andy is now unemployed. Andy hates unemployment, it's boring and soul destroying. All he's ever known is the construction industry and he knows the industry very well. Andy contacted several of his former colleagues who were also made redundant, those people who also know and love the industry and wish to remain within it. Andy and another four guys decide to sit down and come up with a plan together, to establish their own construction company. It's hard work because the economy is slow but every day the five of them are working towards building up this new construction company.

You see, even the unemployed can be attractive, as long as they have ambition and drive.

But even ambition may not be good enough if you are doing nothing about that ambition. Once again, what sets Harry, Kieron and Andy apart is that they all have a plan, written down and they are working towards that plan. One day, they will all make it. There is no way they can't! None of those guys are blaming society, a lack of education, a lack of opportunity, lack of parental help or the fact they were made unemployed for their present position. All these guys have grabbed their lives by the balls and are taking *personal responsibility* for themselves and their position. If they have any failures or setbacks along the way then they will not blame the bank, the economy or anybody else. They will simply learn from it and move on a lot stronger than they were before.

Alpha males take personal responsibility! By relying on other people, the council, the state or other outside forces for your situation; you are giving away all your power to improve your position.

These three guys will succeed and anyone who speaks to them knows this! That is why they are attractive guys! They have ambition. Women love guys who have ambition. It is far more attractive to have an ambitious guy than a guy who has already made it but who wants to progress no further. Those at the top can lose what they have very easily and if they lack that fire and ambition then there will be no way they can ever get back to where they were.

Just like Baz Luhrman said in the song Sunscreen: Never take a lover or a trust fund for granted – You never know when either will run out!

Remember: If you're not growing, you're shrinking because others are growing!

You need to decide where you want to be in life! Have a plan for ten years. Have a plan for 5 years. And finally have a plan for next year.

Actually, physically write down a plan on a sheet of paper and carry it around with you. Look at it every few days and make sure you are taking the measures necessary on that sheet of paper. When you complete them, tick them off.

Studies have shown that by actually having a written plan of your short term goals, you are more likely to achieve them. This is because you are making yourself accountable, to yourself! You are taking *personal responsibility*!

Hopefully you will already know what it is you want to do in life and what your dreams are. If that is the case then you can skip the next section.

What if you don't know what you want to do?

Clearly knowing what your dreams are so you can work towards them is imperative to creating your plan. If you have no idea what you want to be doing with your life then it's important that you take the time to discover it, so that then, finally you can dedicate everything towards getting there.

Take a look at these suggestions for trying to discover what you should be doing.

- Write down the five things you enjoy doing the most. If you have any hobbies such as playing music, drawing, writing or travelling then write them down. Which of the five do you enjoy the most and which of the five have the most viable career options?
- What are you really good at? Do you excel at anything? Do you speak a foreign language well? Is there any extreme sport you're good at? Do you have any special knowledge of any particular subject? Write them down. Are there any careers within this area?
- Are you an expert at anything? Do you have any prior knowledge from former jobs that would qualify you as an expert in a certain area?

- What hobbies have you always wanted to take up but have never gotten round to starting? Are there viable careers within these hobbies?
- What did you really enjoy doing at school? Was there any particular subject you were really good at?
- Imagine you just discovered you only have a year left to live. What do you regret never doing?

Discovering that one thing you want to dedicate everything towards is not easy, I totally understand that. But if you don't yet know what it is, it's very important you dedicate some time and literally have a deep think about what you want from life.

Only once you know what it is can you then go full throttle in that direction and dedicate everything you have to getting there.

Alpha Element # 4

Displays of Expertise

This should be a longer term goal for you!

Becoming an expert on something means that you'll have the ultimate confidence, within yourself at least in this particular field. You should endeavour to become the "go to" man in whatever it is you do!

When you become the "go to" man, then people inevitably flock to you. You'll be invited to more events than you can possibly handle, get to meet more people than is possible and get to make a huge difference in the process.

It doesn't matter what it is, but choose something, something very small and niche if need be and learn absolutely everything you can about it. If your job doesn't allow you to become an expert in that area then think about what your hobbies are? If you like going to the gym then become an expert on cardio or weight training; whichever one you prefer the most. If you like surfing then you should endeavour to not just become as good at surfing as you possibly can, but also learn everything about the sport too so that you would be the perfect person to go to if somebody wanted to learn to surf.

So what else does becoming an expert on something do for you?

Well how many people do you know that are experts at anything?

I'm guessing probably not too many.

Let's say for example you're an expert on creating websites. How many doors will this open for you? How many people could you meet and help out and how much money could you potentially make?

Remember that whatever it is you choose to become an expert in, you need to read as much as possible on the subject but you also need to practice it too. You can read all you want on bodybuilding for example, but you're not going to look like an expert unless you actually hit the gym.

Remember what I was saying earlier with the yoga analogy? Being good at yoga would mean you could walk into any yoga class in the world and appear like a confident individual, even if you didn't consider yourself a confident person? This is the exact same point I'm trying to make. By being an expert on your chosen activity, job or hobby you'll be able to go anywhere in the world and meet with like-minded people and you will still be considered an expert, which will of course make you seem confident. With me, this was breakdancing! What is it with you?

I have a friend who is one of the best people you'll ever find for creating furniture by hand. He can all on his own create from start to finish any type of wooden furniture you can think of. He plans out his projects on paper, buys the correct kind of wood, shapes everything to the correct specifications and puts it all together. If anybody wants anything made from wood, they know who to go to. He gets to meet all kinds of people through what he does and he also gets to travel teaching workshops and giving lectures. This is because he is an expert and people seek out experts.

If you don't have anything then don't fret. The truth is that the vast majority of people are not and never will be an expert on anything. This is what you should see as your medium term goal. So pick something you're passionate about and attack it with everything you have.

Another motivator for becoming an expert is that it has been proven in scientific studies that women highly value expertise. In a study by Clegg, Nettle and Miell in 2011, it was found that from a sample of over 200 visual artists, the more successful artists had more sexual partners than the less successful artists. Interestingly the same thing could not be said for the female artists. This is evidence that while men do not necessarily value expertise and talent, women certainly do!

A study by Aggleton and Baker et al in 2004 found that students of both genders who participated in sports had a significantly higher number of sexual partners than did those students who did not take part in sports. Most interestingly of all however was that within the athletes, a greater level of performance was a predictor for even more sexual partners.

Hasleton and Miller in 2006 compared female preferences towards creative poor men and rich uncreative men. It was found that those women at peak fertility preferred the poor creative men over their richer yet less creative counterparts.

There you have it! This is evidence that becoming an expert in a field, any field is advantageous and consistent with being alpha. There are many more studies showing expertise in a range of categories; I simply picked out three. It really doesn't matter what it is. It stands to reason that if there is a room full of geeky chess players, computer hackers or World of Warcraft enthusiasts; it will be the most talented in these areas who will get the most attention. And that attention won't just be from the men, but from the girls too.

By becoming an expert on something and by meeting experts in other fields, you'll be able to complement the next major element of the alpha male which you'll learn about now.

Alpha Element # 5

Social Proof

Having a high level of social proof will more than make up for deficiencies in other areas. Many people would argue that social proof is the most important element of being an alpha male. I personally would have a hard time arguing with that. If you have social proof, then you will still have insane choice when it comes to women even if you are severely lacking in all the other areas mentioned in this book.

So what is social proof? Social proof or pre-selection is a form of herd behaviour. When somebody is in a situation and is unsure how to behave, they will often look to others for cues as to how to behave. "We conform because we believe that other's interpretation of an ambiguous situation is more accurate than ours and will help us choose an appropriate course of action."

Let me give you a couple of examples. Imagine you are walking down the street and you see a group of twenty or so people staring up into the sky at apparently nothing. What do you do? Do you carry on walking or do you stop and stare up at the sky to see what is about to happen? Of course, the vast majority of people will stop and stare and wait for as long as it takes to see what is about to occur in the sky.

One of the world's greatest violin players decided to busk in a New York subway station at rush hour. He played songs on the world's most expensive violin for a social experiment. After an hour of playing, not a single person stopped to listen and appreciate the great music. Sure a few people dropped in a few coins. But every single person, out of the thousands who must have walked past failed to stop and actually listen to and appreciate the music. What could have happened if even a single person had stopped and listened? This would probably have created a crowd.

Now imagine you're in a bar and an apparently average looking guy walks in accompanied by five beautiful women. What do you think of him? Apart from great envy, you're probably wondering the same as what other women in the bar are thinking. What is so great about that guy?

I will guarantee to you right now, that the easiest way to pick up girls in a bar is to walk in with a number of beautiful women. By doing that you are proving beyond all reasonable doubt that you are an attractive man. This is obvious because you already have the women on your shoulder to prove it. Do you recall the case of the grouse from earlier on in the book? Those alpha grouse receive 80% of all female attention! This is a time saving measure. The fact that certain grouse are surrounded by females when others aren't is proof that certain grouse are much superior mating material. Any women in the bar who see men surrounded by other women will of course be wondering just why this guy is so popular. He is pre-selected. Probably because he is attractive, has a good career, is ambitious, physically fit, is a leader, is not a creep, can be trusted, is an alpha male. This is the kind of guy women are genetically programmed to seek out. If they could somehow meet this guy in the bar surrounded by all the women, then it would save time, money and effort for the women having to "date" in order to find that perfect guy with the right genes to pass down to the next generation.

It's that old rule: If you don't have a girlfriend, it's hard to get one - If you do, they're all over you.

For humans however, the need for social proof is even greater than with grouse. This is for the simple reason that humans are more social than grouse, and all other animals, with a few exceptions.

Now take a guy who is sat alone in the same bar. What message does he send out before he's even opened his mouth? Why does he not have any women around him? What's wrong with him? Why does he have no friends to come out with? He must have a poor career too because he's clearly not a sociable person. Then, imagine that suddenly two guys and four women suddenly enter the bar, find him, walk up to him and hug him because they are clearly his friends. How does your perception change?

Social proof is very powerful!

How To Gain Pre-Selection From Scratch

This is something you should develop over a period of time. Becoming pre-selected is not something like improving your body language where you can do it quickly and easily. It will require work, effort and in many cases considerable time.

It also requires investment in people!

Please read that last line again. The idea is to build your social circle of both men and women, making real friends which cannot be faked.

You have to be a genuine and likeable person, an alpha male who looks out for the people you're with.

So how can you get in with a new group? Well if you've read The Game by Neil Strauss you will know the importance of being indirect when it comes to approaching new groups. But things have evolved now since that excellent book was written. If there were three smaller groups within a larger group, a class at university for example and you wanted to be friends with everybody in group one because they were the cooler group, you may first have to prove your worth by getting to know the slightly less cool group two. However, before you get to know them, you may first have to get to know the even lesser cool group three. Getting to know group three is easy because they are the least cool.

The best thing to do when entering this new extended group would be to get to know the guys in group 3, then the girls. From then on you can work your way up to group two by introducing the guys, but especially the girls to everybody in group two. Then you should establish yourself in group two, beginning with the guys primarily and then the girls. Once you have become established in group two, you can then introduce everybody in group two but especially the girls to everybody in group one, where you always wanted to be. Once you're in group one you begin building a friendship primarily with the guys and then you will be free to get to know the top girls in the top group unhindered.

This very dynamic is what many of the world's top pick up artists will use when they enter night clubs or bars to get to the most attractive women in the venue. They will literally bounce from one group to the next, working their way up every time. This same tactic works just the same in any group situation. If you're at university and you want to hang out in the cool group, then this is the most beneficial way of doing it. If you want to be speaking to the most beautiful girl in your yoga class then it's odds on you're simply not going to be able to walk right up to her and become her friend. She has hundreds of people, men especially falling over themselves to be her friend. It is far better to approach things the other way, like the grouse does.

In any case, chances are that by showing how friendly you are, and by being the guy who is speaking to absolutely everybody, except for her, it's extremely likely she'll seek you out all on her own. This is what happens! Women are programmed to seek out those rare sociable guys that everybody likes.

The method I described above is quite tactical and may read a little underhanded like you're some kind of a spy trying to infiltrate the top group. Well yes, you can think of it that way if you like, but when it comes down to it, what you're actually doing is talking to *everybody*. You're getting to know *everybody*. You're making friends with *everybody*! How many guys do this?

And no, you're not abandoning your former group when you move to the next one. You're taking them with you so that everybody benefits. And it's all down to you!

Ok, we're going to carry on by using yoga as an example as we delve a little further into social proof and expanding our social circle.

As you progress through the groups you really need to be getting to know the people in them. What are their hobbies? What do they do for a living? What do they want to do with their lives (ambitions)? They are three useful things to know about people for building on social proof. Why? Because we all have hobbies, most of us work and we all without exceptions have hopes and dreams for the future.

When you learn these things about people you need to remember them, show you are interested because it's this that will make a huge difference.

Because when you move from group three to group two it will be extremely beneficial for everybody if you're able to connect two people from different groups together. If John from group three likes to go snowboarding and Harry from group two would like to learn, or is just getting into snowboarding, then those two can connect through you. If Mary from group one is in bad need of a highly qualified electrician and you know that David from group two just happens to do that for a living then you can connect the two of them up.

What you're doing is bringing people together, improving lives and everything is done through you! The alpha male! It takes no time at all to connect people together and it doesn't cost a penny.

Within a short space of time, your social circle will be expanding. This goes without saying that of course, you can connect people from different groups too, not just the groups within the groups, if that makes sense. So you can connect your yoga friends with your work colleagues should the desire arise.

By intentionally going out of your way to benefit others, the rewards will come back in abundance. Remember, it takes little time and costs nothing but you are improving the lives of those people around you.

Alpha males look out for their people!

Remember the lions in the jungle? It is the responsibility of the alpha to provide for and to look after the health and safety of the rest of the pack.

Expect to have your group introduce you to others from outside. Just as you have been doing for them, they will do for you. How many of those women that you're not attracted to but who you've been going out of the way to connect with somebody to teach her piano lessons will have attractive friends that maybe you will be interested in.

If somebody new shows up on the scene of any of your groups (yoga, work, snowboarding etc) it will be you who has the power to bring this new person into the fold. What does this new person do for hobbies? What is their job? What does he/she want to do with their lives? If it's the dream of this new person who showed up at your yoga class to become a reporter for example and you just happen to know somebody in human resources at the local newspaper, then I'm already sure you know what to do.

Have a think about your life right now?

How many people truly go out of their way to bring people together, help each other out and ask for nothing in return? Not many at all!

As I said at the beginning of this book, being an alpha male is about being the best possible guy you can be. The kind of guy that women want to be around.

If you combine social proof with leadership, which we are moving on to now, then pretty soon, you will be the guy walking into a bar with five women.

Alpha Element # 6

Leadership

When you think about it, the word *leader* is really just another word for *organiser*.

Have a think about any alpha males or leaders you know. Are they all organisers too? Are they the people who ring around your group to arrange when and where to meet up and what to do? Who are those people you know who gather all your friends together to meet up at your local bar? Usually it's the alpha male right?

Alpha males lead! Alpha males organise!

Leadership ability is one of the most important reasons why *certain* people get promotions at work in front of those others who are less able to lead or organise. Organising ability is valued. Having the ability to instruct other people and to get the best out of them will give you much better prospects throughout your career.

So this yoga class you attend every Wednesday, who is the guy, or girl who organises the social events? Who is the person who tells everybody else the class is getting together for its first ever meet up outside of class to get to know each other a little better?

Nobody I hear you say?

Well then this could be your chance to establish yourself as the organiser, the leader, the alpha!

You should have already established yourself within the group (see social proof above) and so organising a night out for a few drinks, or a meal at a nice restaurant should be fairly straightforward for you to accomplish.

Don't wait around for somebody else in the group to organise a gathering. You must take the initiative to do it yourself. After all, that is what everybody else is waiting to happen. They are waiting for somebody else to organise an outing to make more interesting their lives. You need to be this person!

Have belief that you can do this and you'll surprise yourself. Remember that people are sociable creatures. They need human interaction and you're going to give them it!

When deciding where to go or what to do, the best thing you can decide is to do the one thing that benefits *yourself* and the *group* as a whole. You'll never please everybody all of the time, but you can certainly please the majority. In order to please the majority of people you'll have to have a think about what the majority of the people in your group likes. This could be fairly easy depending on what your group is; yoga, work, Italian cooking class etc.

Then when you have a good idea of your chosen activity, be *decisive*! Alpha males are decisive! Don't ask what they would rather do; go to the new Italian restaurant in town or to the new Indian restaurant. Say that there is a new Italian restaurant in town and you are setting up a meal for the group. If you take away any choice or responsibility for the group members then you decrease the chances of non-compliance, or in this case, not showing up. This is because most people by their nature are followers and not leaders so if you give them work to do (making up their minds) then most people will simply defer to you anyway. However, you are the alpha male, you have already put thought into it and you've decided for everybody that the new Italian would be great for everybody. If nobody has any thought (work) to put into the decision and you are decisive then you will get many accepted invitations.

One of the world's most famous pick up artists became well-known for his social proof innovations within the field. It was not unknown for him to enter bars with 100+ women. With such a huge social circle, one can clearly make magic happen. It was his rule to never hit on any of the women in his entourage; he needed their trust after all for his true pick up method to come to fruition. Imagine the impact any guy who enters a club with that kind of social proof would have on the thoughts of the other women in there. He never needed to pick up any women or do any work to try and get anybody interested in him. All the hottest women in the clubs would always approach him, just to find out what all the fuss was about.

Many years after perfecting this strategy, which he called Entourage Game, he explained exactly how he was able to turn up at a bar on a Monday, Tuesday, Wednesday, Thursday, Friday, Saturday or Sunday evening with over a hundred hot women.

He simply created his own club for women, where he would show them round the best bars in town, with the promise of cutting the queue and walking straight in along with the promise of an awesome night out. I suppose arriving to any bar with a hundred women also granted him favours with management (VIP treatment etc). He did it all through Facebook. Visitors in town, desiring a night out could find his service and he delivered.

He showed leadership and it paid off for him!

Now, you don't have to create your own giant club for party goers; that was just an extreme example of what is possible. But everybody has hobbies! There is nothing stopping you from creating your own club or society within your own area and getting together with like-minded people; with you as the organiser.

Whatever your hobby is in this world, you will be able to find people to hang out with whether it be surfing, poker, diving, swimming, running, clubbing, stamp collecting or something I've not even heard about.

In the age of Facebook it is easier than ever before to create groups of people with similar interests in and around the area you live. There is nothing stopping you from creating a Facebook Tennis Manchester group or a Boston Sprinting group.

Create the group > Meet up > Do your chosen activity > Organise social gatherings

Nobody is going to do it for you. You have to take the initiative, be the alpha male and create it yourself. It's easy!

Alpha Element # 7

Ability to Connect

Alpha males are master communicators! This is because alpha males are forever surrounded by people so they are well versed in getting along with all kinds of people. The alpha male is almost always almost immediately liked.

How can he do this? It's through his superior communication and ability to connect with others.

The alpha male is able to make other people feel alive and special when he's in their presence.

If you are able to connect well with people, then you will always be loved by everybody you come across.

When I think about all the master communicators throughout history, the one who springs to mind is Admiral Horatio Nelson. Nelson was an extremely short, sickly looking man from having contracted malaria as a young boy. He lost an arm in one battle and an eye in another. Despite being the Vice Admiral of the entire British navy Nelson still insisted on being the first man to board enemy ships during battle, despite having only one arm and only being 5'4" in height.

But it was his ability to communicate in an extraordinary manner which really made him loved by his men. Nelson would treat all his men the same, no matter what their rank and was extremely concerned with their general health and well-being. Nelson showed a great personal interest in his men as individuals throughout his career as well as an ability to imaginatively engage with their particular needs and problems.

It was said that when you spoke to Nelson, it was like you were the only person that mattered on earth. In fact when Nelson was shot by a sniper at the battle of Trafalgar in 1805, many of his men, hardened seamen, broke down and cried.

How did Nelson communicate in this way, in a way that had such a profound effect on everybody he came across? You will find out below. The very first book I wrote a number of years ago was *First Date Tips for Men*. I will now lift a section from that book entitled Establishing a Connection. Please keep in mind that this piece was written with the first date in mind, establishing a connection with women. However, while yes this is what it is for, the same principles can and should be used for establishing connections with men as well and in any situation you can think of.

Start VVV

It is getting a connection with a girl that is the single most important thing you could ever have in order to make it to a second date! In fact if you get this right then you won't really need anything else in this guide! Everything else would just be a bonus!

Connection is the reason why ugly guys get to sleep with very attractive girls!

Connection is the reason why so many guys end up marrying their existing female friends! Friends they weren't initially even attracted to! You do after all fall in love with the person and not the looks right?

Unfortunately for connection, it takes a long, long time in many cases to build!

But what if there was a way to build instant connection? What if there was a way to have a girl fall in love with you almost immediately, or very quickly?

Is this possible?

I'm sure you've heard girls say about their boyfriend or husband that there was this instant connection and they just hit if off right away!

Fortunately this can happen and lucky guys can indeed fluke it!

But what if there was a way to get an instant connection with any girl and almost straight away?

Fortunately for you you're reading this guide!

You can build a connection with a girl by communicating directly with her innermost thoughts, desires, beliefs, motivations and experiences!

Read that last paragraph again!

If she believes that you understand her on these levels, these innermost levels which lie beneath her skin and deep in her head then there's no way that she's not going to feel incredibly close to you!

In general; men are not very good at this kind of thing, but girls are! This is why girls can often hit it off with each other right from the start!

Have you ever found yourself in a situation where you're telling someone, a guy for example about yourself at a party or wherever and you suddenly find yourself telling him even more about yourself simply because he comes across as being interested in what you have to say?

This is very hard to explain unless you can relate to it yourself!

Now I'm going to give you a few example conversations starting with how not to build a connection and slowly improve the conversation up until where finally, you should be building incredible connection with the girl:

Conversation 1

Guy: So what are your hobbies?

Girl: Well I really like to go horse riding in my spare time, I've been riding ever since I was a little girl and we had horses on the farm!

Guy: Oh I don't really know anything about horse riding, what else are you into?

Funny as that may sound, this is what 99% of guys actually do when meeting new people!

Conversation 2

Guy: So what are your hobbies?

Girl: Well I really like to go horse riding in my spare time, I've been riding ever since I was a little girl and we had horses on the farm!

Guy: Oh I had a friend who goes horse riding, yeah she loves it! You two would probably get on great!

This is a little bit better, at least this guy is trying to form a bond! But why would she care about his friend that goes horse riding? She's never met her and probably never will! Most guys do this and I'm sure you have in the past.

Now let's look at a situation where the guy is at least relating the girls answer to her:

Conversation 3

Guy: So what are your hobbies?

Girl: Well I really like to go horse riding in my spare time, I've been riding ever since I was a little girl and we had horses on the farm!

Guy: Wow so you're a horse rider? That's impressive! I would never have thought that about you when I first saw you!

Girl: Why would you say that?

Guy: I'm very impressed, I just can't picture you as the kind of girl who'd be such the outdoorsy type! Wow! Now you have my attention!

Now this is so much better. There's even a bit of banter in there, he's being playful and they're having a good time. If you even did this you'd be so far ahead of nearly every single guy on the planet. But you could take it even further and relate what she's saying even more to her!

Conversation 4

Guy: So what are your hobbies?

Girl: Well I really like to go horse riding in my spare time, I've been riding ever since I was a little girl and we had horses on the farm!

Guy: Wow! So you're a horse rider? I'm impressed, now you've got my attention! I would never have pictured you as the outdoorsy type when I first saw you, but it just goes to show you can never tell! You must really care for horses, and I've heard they're such a high maintenance animal to have, you must be an incredibly caring person. You must love the feeling of riding a horse at high speed through the fields? Tell me how that feels!

Now I know nothing about horses! But I've taken something that she says she's passionate about and I've related it to her! You really don't need to know anything about horses to be able to do this!

> When adults talk about things that happened in both their childhoods an instant connection is formed!
>
> A very common theme is children's television!
>
> How often do you talk about your favourite TV programs as a child and end up feeling a connection with that person even if you've never spoken to them before?

> If you could take the same principle but apply it to something more than TV then you have a secret weapon you can use to your advantage!
>
> Try and find out if you had shared hobbies as kids!
>
> Did she go to girl guides as you went to boy scouts? Did you attend any similar sports or athletics clubs? Did you know any of the same people when you were younger? If you went to the same school then you will have known the same teachers! Did you go on holiday to the same place as children?
>
> Knowing this information, you can use it to create an incredibly strong bond very easily!

Horse riding is her passion and I've made a connection with her about horse riding and shown I'm interested! She'll no doubt be willing to talk for a long time about horse riding and all the guy in conversation 4 has to do is look like he's really interested and connect on any more points made.

Now let's take another example of connecting:

Guy: You look very exotic, where is it you're from?

Girl: I'm from two miles up the street!

Guy: Very funny! But your parents...they must be from somewhere far, far away?

Girl: Haha yes, my Father is from France and my Mother is Italian!

Guy: Oh that's pretty cool! I've never been to Europe myself but I'm a big fan of Italian culture! They have a history that's just so remarkable and the Italian people are so proud of being Italian. It really shows in them I think! And you're half French too? That must mean you're really good at cooking then! I bet you're also a really fiery person who mustn't be messed with! I bet you've been to France lots of times?

Now most of the above is just me rambling on!

But the important thing is that I'm making a connection.

She's going to like the idea of being a "fiery person" and there's just no way she's going to disagree with being "proud!"

I would expect the girl to spend a good considerable time talking about France or Italy! And you should let her! Don't interrupt! She feels she can trust you because you've got this instant connection!

Ok, so let's take another example around something that's very important to all of us. We'll start with what happens on most occasions and then we'll improve from there out.

Guy: So what is it you do?

Girl: I'm at university studying to become a nurse!

Guy: Oh I've a friend who's a nurse. She lives in...

Once again, the average guy in this conversation is immediately relating HER career to HIMSELF! This really is the default position that most guys take instinctively which causes girls to wonder why they bother telling them anything at all.

Let's try again.

Guy: So what is it you do?

Girl: I'm at university studying to become a nurse!

Guy: OK that's cool! That must mean you're a genuinely kind and caring person! You must just love helping people.

Girl: Yeah, I suppose I do! Yeah you're right about that!

Guy: So, tell me, I'm interested…What is it about being a nurse that you like so much?

When you take something like career, hobbies or interests and then you ask them what it is they like about that thing, you're really getting deep down into the girls mind. This is how you form close bonds with people.

Girl: Hmm I've never been asked that before. Well I suppose I like helping people, I get home and I know I've made a difference in a few people's lives. That makes me feel good.

Guy: Looks like I was right! You really are a kind and caring person aren't you!

What I would do now is reread this section again. Run through it in your own mind and get it down to an art! If you can master communicating with women on this level, then your first date will feel to her like you've known each other for a very long time.

You're now becoming an unstoppable machine in the dating world! From now on everything else you're going to read in this guide is an added bonus!

End ^^^

Alpha Element # 8

Life Experiences

In my book Confidence for Men; one of the main pieces of advice I give to guys to become more confident is to gain life experiences. Many different and interesting life experiences! I then gave a long list of practical things guys can realistically do to help them become confident.

Remember when I said we become confident in different areas through competence. Well by achieving enough competence in many different areas, one can reasonably expect to become a confident person throughout their life.

You know all those people who appear super confident because they're chatting away to all their friends about having gone sky diving over the weekend, or because they've just come back from a year away travelling, or because they have a cool story to tell about how they just got a girl's phone number, or because they've just stood in front of two hundred people and made a speech, or because they've just started attending drama classes, or because they've just climbed a mountain, or because they've just camped out in the wilderness, or because they've just cycled from one end of the country to the other or because they've just learnt how to hang glide.

What do these people have in common?

They are all getting out there and living their lives! They are having fun! They are meeting people! They are telling their stories! They are experiencing life to the full!

Alpha males are exciting and interesting because they have life experiences and they can draw people in partly because of this.

Everybody has a long list of things in their heads that they really want to get round to doing at some point in their lives. However, alpha males actually go out there and do these things! They don't sit back and think about it, they just get up and do it!

Alpha males are action takers!

What are those things you have always wanted to do but never had the inclination to look in to. Write a list of those things, trust me, actually seeing them written down in front of you is the first step, having them in your head is not.

After writing them down, choose those activities that you can do *now*! Make a commitment to yourself to do them!

For me, the thing I always wanted to do was learn to breakdance! So I went out and did it! Many of my best friends are break dancers and I've had relationships with girls through that activity. What is your chosen activity? You will meet your best friends in life through hobbies that you share in common.

I didn't stop at break dancing however. I always wanted to learn Italian due to an obsession with that country, so not only did I learn to speak the language, but I also spent a whole month travelling throughout Italy.

Now I'm a little too old to breakdance any more so I am starting my own running class. Remember HIIT (High Intensity Interval Training) that I was telling you about? I am now starting a class in my area, three times a week where we do HIIT in the local park.

Imagine the stories I'll be able to tell new people I meet about running my own HIIT class, where I guarantee everybody who attends will lose weight faster than any other method. Imagine the amount of people I'll meet by running my own running class three evenings a week. As I mentioned earlier, we'll also no doubt be having frequent evening socials.

Last year I went out on my bike and cycled along the canal. I didn't stop until I reached the end...In Liverpool, 140 miles away! Then I cycled back. It took me a little more than a day and a night to complete. That's another life experience I can tick off the list and I could talk for an hour about the day I did that, the things I saw and experienced, the pain I felt.

If there's something I am interested in doing then I plan it out and I do it! I certainly don't waste time playing on the Playstation. I don't spend all my time in bed. I am getting out there and living my life.

Remember, I used to be the guy who hid my face behind my hair and now I'm teaching running classes.

Now I'm the guy who appears super confident because I can hold a group of people with my stories about breakdancing, travelling, Italy, HIIT, doing spontaneous cycling trips and soon to be hang gliding.

It really is that simple!

Have some life experiences!

Part 3

Alpha Extras

Be On A Pedestal

Alpha males know they are the man! They have this belief about themselves! People know an alpha male even before they've opened their mouths. I'm sure you already know this. Next time you see a group of guys together, have a guess who the alpha is; it's easy.

But alpha males don't go around saying "I'm awesome!" If they were awesome then why would they need to go around telling everybody?

No, alpha males are awesome and indeed are the people everybody wants to be around because of all of the above; physical attraction, confidence, ambition, displays of expertise, social proof, leadership, ability to connect and life experience.

There are no tricks to it! It's all about being the best possible person you can be. When you do this, people will flock towards you, look up to you and expect amazing things from you.

However, there are still a few tricks you can use to put yourself on a pedestal over and above other people. This technique I'm going to explain to you can best be used to get women to chase you, because you're demonstrating that you're slightly above them, you're demonstrating yourself to be a challenge and so they will rise to that challenge and chase you. This technique is called qualification and since qualification is relevant to being an alpha male, I'm going to lift the section on qualification from my book First Date Tips for Men.

Start VVV

Now I'm tempted to say that qualification is even more important than forging a connection with the girl, but for the simple reason that you won't get to qualification or really even need it if you build a good connection, I'm still putting the earlier section at the top of my list.

Once again, I will reiterate that building a connection is the most important thing to make a girl want to see you again.

But let's change the mind set for this section. For qualification is where YOU decide if you want to see HER again.

Qualification is something women are very, very good at!

They do it naturally! They do it all the time simply because they grow up with an expectation of what their dream guy should be like! Even if later on in their lives they become realistic as to what men actually are, when they are younger, girls still have this high expectation of what they want in a boyfriend or of men in general.

In fact it's tough luck for any guy who doesn't meet this high expectation.

In fact it's become a lot harder for us guys to "qualify" to their high expectations all thanks to Sex and the City and countless romantic comedies starring Jennifer Aniston, but I won't bore you by ranting on about that!

To put it simply, girls have in their heads a list of what we have to be like in order for them to be interested in us. It usually looks something like this:

1. Sense of humour
2. He MUST be a Doctor, Lawyer or run his own successful business
3. He must get me
4. He must be caring and sensitive
5. He must have an incredible body
6. He must be handsome
7. All my friends must also love him

This list will probably run on and on. The thing is that the hotter the girl, in most cases the longer the list.

In fact, girls will often go out of their way to find this information out about us and they'll be completely unapologetic about it too!

Take a typical conversation on the average first date:

Girl: So what is it you do?

Guy: I'm doing an apprenticeship with Auto Mechanics in town! / I work for the tax department / I'm an administrator!

Girl: Oh so how long have you been doing that?

Guy: About 2 years!

Girl: But you're also at Uni as well right? You are aiming for higher things yes?

Guy: Ermm well errmmm no.

In fact the guy above sensing the girls disappointment with what he does, seeing he could now lose her has to try hard to make up lost ground! But it's already too late!

Once he has to try to get her to like him again, it's already game over in most situations!

She has qualified him to her expectations and he did not match up to what she wants in a man!

The only way I can see him turning this around would be to show how proud he is of doing what he's doing. Showing how he's making a difference etc. Then bide his time and qualify her to HIS standards!

This is often hard for us guys! Remember her list above? Well this is a typical guys list:

    1. She must be hot!

Is it any wonder why girls have a big advantage over us? Is it any wonder why it so often appears like it's them that get to do all the picking and choosing instead of us guys!

Qualification is something that all women do! The hotter the woman the worse it gets!

But what if we could play them at their own game? What if we could qualify them to our ridiculously high standards of what we need in a woman for us to even consider them?

Well fortunately this is very easy once you understand the principles! We can play them at their own game and frustrate the hell out of them in the process!

You will find that if you're dating a not so hot girl, you won't need to apply much qualification. But trust me, as they get hotter, the more you'll need to qualify them!

If you're dating a girl who dates lots of guys, this is going to make you stand out so far and above any other guy she's ever met!

The first thing we need to do is make a list, just like how they have! You don't have to actually write it down, but just know what it is you want in a girl.

I mean it! What do you actually want in a girl?

This only really works if it's something not related in the slightest to her looks! Make sure that you're the only guy she's ever met who couldn't give a damn about her looks! The looks are just a bonus! What you really want, what you really need in a girl is what you have on your list!!!

1. She must be ambitious!
2. She mustn't smoke!

3. She must not be the one who simply follows all her mates, but does her own thing.

4. She can hold a conversation.

5. She's clever.

6. She likes to travel and discover new places.

7. She can't be materialistic. I need a girl who can be happy without all those flashy things.

8. She has to be spontaneous! I need someone who can run out in the rain with me when it thunders and just go crazy!

You see what a list like this does?

It doesn't matter how attractive she is! If she doesn't tick your boxes on this list then she doesn't get a look in! You'll be the only guy she's ever known who would turn her down simply because she's not spontaneous!

Hot girls are used to having all the power!

Now you've just taken that power away from her!

And because of this, she has no choice but to chase YOU!!!

And she WILL chase you!!!

She'll chase you because you're different, you're the only guy she's ever met that isn't drooling over her!

You're the only guy she's ever met who's used qualification!!!

So...now you have your list! How best to use this list?

Well the best way to use this magical list is to be blunt and just ask her!

Remember that the contents of this list are very important to you. So why not just ask her? She asked you about your job right? So play her at her own game!

Guy: You know, you're quite funny which I really like and you can hold a conversation! But what I really want to know is if you're the kind of girl who just loves discovering new places?

You need to make it look like it's important to you!

Disclaimer: You need to have built up a certain amount of rapport and have made at least some connection before using this! Otherwise she's not going to care whether she conforms to your standards or not!

No girl in the world is going to say "no" she doesn't like discovering new places! The fact is it doesn't matter! You're qualifying her based on something other than her looks and so far she's passing your tests!

After this initial little bit of qualification I would wait a while before trying it again. You could in the meantime find out what places she's discovered recently! And I'm not talking about the new nail painting place down the road!

By getting her to "explain herself" to you, by trying to impress you by telling you of the places she's discovered, you're forcing her to make a big effort to impress you.

Wait a few minutes and then throw in the big one, the money shot, the deal breaker!

Girl: So that's where I always go to get my nails done these days!

Guy: That's fine! Are you spontaneous??? I really like spontaneous people!!!

Again, no girl in the world is going to say she's not spontaneous. Even most guys like to think of themselves as being spontaneous, it is after all another word for exciting is it not?

Let's go back to the conversation where we left off!

Girl: Oh well erm, yes I suppose I am spontaneous!!!

Guy: Awesome! Tell me one really spontaneous thing you've done in the last six months?

Now just sit back and wait for her reply!

Remember to make it look like it's important to you that she's spontaneous. It has to seem to her like it's possible that the answer she gives might disappoint you. And that is an extremely important part of it!

If she gives a typical girly answer which is not something that excites you then you need to act genuinely disappointed (breaking rapport)!

Girl: Well I was bored last week so I just phoned my friend up and we drove 50 miles to the next town for a shopping trip!

Guy: That's rubbish! Give me something else! Something really cool that's going to impress me!

Girl: OK well a few weeks ago I was walking by a sign that said "join up for fencing lessons" and I thought, that's so cool, I've just got to give it a go, so I did!

The important thing is that if it sounds genuinely impressive, then you need to be impressed and you need to let her know how cool it is that she did what she did and that she has your approval!

Equally important is that if it's a load of crap and you're not impressed one bit then you have to tell her that that's nothing (in a half jokey, yet half serious way) and she's going to have to try harder to come up with something a little better!

Seriously! What you're doing is getting HER to impress YOU!

Think about all the times there's been girls you've liked in the past. You've gone out of your way to impress them by boasting about your exploits and everything else. What this tends to do in most cases is turn the girl off.

By the very fact that you're trying so hard to impress the girl, shows that she has you in her control, she has very little she needs to do to get you.

By phrasing your questions correctly and by being a little manipulative, you're actually turning the tables and getting her to impress you. Don't be turned off though like she would. You've been very clever and so you should reap the rewards.

When we try hard to impress somebody, it's because we really like them! We try to impress people because we want them to like us too. Qualification is how you get them to try and impress YOU, because on a deep down level you've positioned yourself slightly above them and they need to demonstrate that they are on your level.

By using qualification on a girl you're pretty much, for lack of a better expression, forcing her to impress you. If she's trying to impress you, then she must clearly like you!

This is how the rich ugly guy gets the gorgeous girl. Because rich guys naturally use qualification all the time. They've already been there and done that, they've got the car to prove it. If a girl is even to get a look in, then they're going to have to prove they're worth the effort.

One thing about girls, especially really hot girls is that they're very competitive! They have huge egos and this is how you use it to your advantage!

End ^^^

Yes, I wrote that piece with the first date in mind. By using qualification in that way on a first date and even beyond you will have the girl chasing you for sure. That is also how you can get guys to try and impress you in much the same way.

I included the above piece because it clearly shows the inner workings of an alpha male. If you can use qualification from a genuine perspective and not one of manipulation then you have a very powerful tool at your disposal.

It's no use asking women you're interested in if they love to travel if you don't love it yourself. It's no good asking women if they love to travel if you are not yourself in fact well-travelled. In most instances women will ask you where you have travelled to, after you have asked them, and if you've never been outside your state or country, spent a night in the wilderness, climbed that mountain or cycled cross country then it's not going to work, in fact it may well back fire on you.

We are not using psychological tricks here; we are trying to be the very best people we can be, so that women will naturally want to be with us. If you become this interesting person then you'll end up using qualification naturally without even knowing it for the people who come in to your life to be worth your time and effort. Just ask the ugly rich guy who you see walking down the street with a gorgeous girl. He has her not because of his money, but because he has high standards and for people to get close to him, they have to conform to his standards, which means they have to chase him. It's an ego thing for women! Especially the hotter women who tend to have much bigger egos!

Most guys who would buy a book like this one, and I thank you very much for doing so, and even more so for wanting to improve yourself to such a high extent, do so because they have standards. Or at least they really want to have those standards. They expect high standards from the women they would date. So if you expect women to have such high standards for you to be interested in them, then you had better make damn sure that you have those high standards yourself, otherwise it's never going to work for you.

This is why I cannot emphasise enough that you need to give up your Playstation, Xbox, Wii, lying in your bed at the weekend and all the rest of the things that men, real men should have given up by now.

You need get out there and start experiencing life and becoming that high value alpha male. It doesn't come from reading alpha male books, but from taking the action I've set out for you in this book.

Take another look at that list you wrote of those things you wanted to do. Pick one and do it this weekend. As for me; as soon as I've finished this book, I'm off to climb Ben Nevis, the highest mountain in the UK.

Raise Your Social Standards

Take a look in the mirror at your default facial expression. How does it look? Happy, sad, indifferent?

Remember at the beginning of this book how I explained how women tend to do most of the approaching me now. That's because I look and come over as being approachable.

Does your default face look approachable? Would you approach you if you were a girl who liked the look of you?

You're probably wondering just why I'm including a section on your default facial expression; how you look when you're sitting down, eating, talking or working.

Take a look at those faces around you while they sit on the train, while they eat dinner, while they work at their desks or while they sit watching TV. This is how people spend the vast majority of their waking lives looking.

The fact is the vast majority of people spend most of their waking lives looking outright miserable! And although 100% of all sane people on this planet thrive on love and attention, we still spend our lives with a face that just says "stay away from me!"

Do you see the problem here?

Those people who are doing really well in their lives and who love life, they tend to walk around with an expression that says they love life. Alpha males walk around with an expression that says "I love life," or "I am on top of the world and nothing is going to bring me down."

It really doesn't take much effort to create a little smile while you're out and about and it will make a big difference to how you feel in yourself as well.

So why don't more people walk around smiling, or using facial animation when they speak, or being expressive with their gestures?

It's because people are terrified that other people won't respond to their happiness!

Do you see the problem? The vast majority of people are prisoners to the thoughts and opinions of others. This is extremely tragic, especially considering that 99.99% of people we walk by every day, we'll never see again. Yet these people have full control over our lives. How very tragic!

Imagine you're sitting on the tube, notice how everybody conforms to the lowest common denominator, how everybody matches the mood of the most miserable person on the tube. God forbid anybody who smiles. It's just like when at school; the whole class is forced to go along at the pace of the slowest child. Those at the bottom drag everybody else downwards.

Well if you haven't noticed already, it's the job of the alpha male to lead! The alpha male breaks the mould and does his own thing. He is the guy who stands out in the crowd. He smiles while everybody else looks sad. When they zig, he zags. When the sheep go one way, you go the other. Sheep are nice because they are easy to predict, so it should be easy for us to stand out.

Being alpha depends on the ability to lead! Being alpha depends on the ability to make choices not based on what other people are doing. Being alpha means doing what's right for you even if it means other people sat in the tube will wonder why you're smiling. Is it right for you to walk around looking like you're enjoying yourself? That's what it means to be alpha! We do our own thing and we don't care what other people think!

Don't adapt to the world around you, but make the world adapt to you!

> *"The reasonable man adapts himself to the world; the unreasonable one persists in trying to adapt the world to himself. Therefore all progress depends on the unreasonable man."* – George Bernard Shaw

This means having to raise your standards. This means having to do those little things that have unfortunately become taboo these days. Heaven forbid that you smile as you walk around. Heaven forbid that you say hello to people when you're in the coffee shop or on the tube.

What's the very worst thing that can happen by saying hello? The very worst thing that can happen is that you will be ignored. That is it!

But what is the best thing that can happen? Maybe you'll get women approaching you because you're different to 99.99% of the other men.

Raising your social standards means you're not just pulling yourself up by the bootstraps and raising yourself above the crowd. It also means you're expecting those closest to you to come with you too.

If the people around you suddenly start to find that you're becoming more confident, getting more attention from men, women and other groups, then it is highly likely they are going to feel left behind.

It is most likely your present peers will do one of two things: 1. They will be happy for you. 2. They will indeed feel left behind and envious of your progress and will be unhappy for themselves. Jealousy is the best word for it!

This also provides you with two options. Hopefully, you'll be able to take your friends with you on the journey and help to improve their lives too. This of course will mean that they will have to put work into themselves, put down the Playstation and embrace the journey. Friends that are happy for you when you are doing better than they are, are actually true friends who're hard to come by.

However, if they refuse to be happy for you, they are going to drag you down. You can't raise your social standards when you're still spending time with people who are bringing you down. Alpha males don't put up with crap from anybody!

I hope you'll be able to stick with your old true friends as you start meeting many new people, in fact you really need to put in the extra effort for all those people who've always been there for you. However, you also need to be prepared to let them go if they prove to be a barrier between you becoming the guy you want to be.

People, women in particular tend to notice how those around us treat us and interact with us. You may be able to fake being an alpha male, at least for a short period of time, but as soon as your new people meet your old people and see your interactions then that's how they'll know straight away whether you're a desirable kind of guy or not.

Do the people you know really well treat you with respect? Or do they talk down to you, bad mouth you, cause you problems and heartache?

If these people aren't going to shape up, then you need to drop them. The alpha male does not need to put up with taking crap from people, especially those who will drag him down. You can't raise your social standards whilst old people are dragging you down and we all know people who would fit this description.

If they are dear to you then give them a final warning. Be the alpha, take charge and tell them straight. You are not going to take this crap any longer. Then if it continues, then you need to be willing to follow through with your word.

Before long, you'll be surrounded with high quality, high value people who in turn will raise you up a few pegs, as you will do for them. We are products of our environments, so we need to create those environments ourselves. Aim for excellence and nothing less. Create an environment for yourself that other people want to be a part of; women in particular. You now know everything you need to do in order to create an atmosphere of yourself and around yourself that will draw other, high quality people towards you.

Spotting If Women Like You

This is also important to being able to get women to approach you, although not imperative. Think of it as a bonus technique you can use to come across as being completely different to all the other guys.

Alpha males get admiring glances from females all the time. Absolutely aaaaaalllllllllllllll the time! You're going to have to live with that I'm afraid!

But if you're interested in the women making admiring glances then you have to be a man, an alpha and make an approach on her. I cover all about the best way of making direct approaches to women during the daytime in my book Direct Day Game Method. I'll include a snippet in a bit.

As guys, we tend to stare at women we're attracted to, sometimes we do it a little too much. But women don't act in the same way because it's not socially acceptable for them to do that. But what they will do is give you quick glances in the hope to catch your eye. When that happens, hold contact and smile. When they smile back...

...Bang!

That is your signal, so don't waste any time. Just get over there.

If women are interested in you, they are no more subtle than that! That is a "come on" invitation for you to make your approach. Alpha males approach women! It's our job! Don't disappoint!

I urge you to take a look at Direct Day Game Method as I explain step by step the easiest pick up routine known to man, the direct method.

But what about all the other women who don't give us the invitation to approach them? Well thankfully, there is a method which I call pre-approach priming. This is something you can do from the other side of the room without risking being shot down in public, not that alpha males care about that. Here is a snippet from Direct Day Game Method.

Start VVV

Pre approach priming (PAP) is not something that you'll be able to carry out all that often during the day time. It is something that is perhaps a little more suited to night game. That is not to say you cannot use it during the day, it's just a little trickier.

Direct day game involves approaching women cold, meaning that you've had no prior contact with them. By using PAP you are warming your approach up a tiny bit in order to increase the chances of having a successful approach.

PAP can be something that is as small as eye contact, to a smile, eye contact and a smile or even a hello or a wave. This is something that many women will even instigate.

So why would women instigate what I call PAP?

Because they want you to approach them!

It's just not the done thing for women to approach guys, that's not how things work unfortunately for us. But that's not to say that women can't give guys subtle signals which are intended to invite us to approach them. This is in fact something that women do on a regular basis. In fact when you're out and about, you should become aware of any PAP signals women are sending you.

When you're walking around, try and make eye contact with as many attractive women as you can. Keep an eye out for those who match your eye contact and smile! That is your invitation to go and approach! You should not hesitate, just do it!

In fact because you've been invited to make the approach, you can even skip the direct opener itself and just go straight up to her and introduce yourself. I've done this many, many times in the street, in the shopping mall and in the best place of all for this; the coffee shop.

You can even take things a step further while in the coffee shop. You can make eye contact with her right from the other side of the room, smile and even wave to her. Trust me, if she waves back, which she most often will do then that is your invite to just casually walk up to her and take the seat opposite.

I read a study somewhere, I wish I could remember where it was, but it was discovered that toddlers who can't yet speak bond much quicker with people they've been waving to across the play pen. If you can get into a "conversation" across the room using any kind of none verbal communication, you're already going to feel very attached to the girl when you sit down next to her, and the feeling will be mutual. Just take the seat and introduce yourself, there's no need for any openers!

You can see how this would work in a bar too, through the loud music, sometimes none verbal communication is the only way forward.

You can see why this perhaps doesn't carry over to the street very well because you're both in motion but if you can just get some eye contact and a smile from her (you must smile first, or say hi as you pass) then this should be all you need. Your approach is no longer cold and you've set yourself up for an extremely warm reception when you turn round, run up to her and say hi!

PAP is something you can also use in the gym if you happen to make eye contact with a girl. You can simply motion something with your arms, perhaps you could pretend to bench press thin air, or just simply wave to her. Bang, you've just warmed up an approach.

If you're waiting to cross the street and there's a hot girl on the other side of the road, then simply tap your watch and make a big yawning gesture, as if to say "I'm tired of waiting here." Seriously, when was the last time a guy did this with her?

The best thing is that it takes zero balls to do this! And the other thing is that if any PAP signals you send out to the girl are not reciprocated then you really haven't lost anything, you haven't even made an approach.

Be creative with your PAP's! Tailor them to your situation and have fun with them. If the girl can see you're smiling and having fun with it, making signals to her from across the crowded coffee shop then she really is going to be open to you when you take the seat opposite her. You're already in a coffee shop too (assuming that's where you are) so I guess you can call this an instant date too.

End ^^^

There you go! It really is that easy, it just takes a little imagination.

Just do this a few times without even approaching her if you've never made any cold approaches during the day time. I've had women start talking to me because I never approached them after making the gesture. Meeting women does not get any easier than that.

I included this section because if you do everything I suggested in this book, making yourself an all-round better person to be around, then you're going to start to notice women doing this to you a lot! It would be a shame to miss out on potential dates because you're not prepared for when it happens.

Quick Fire Questions

Question: What are those beta male behaviours I should avoid?

Well firstly, I don't like the term "beta male," I've not even used it in this book for that reason. Alpha males have no reason to speak of another man as a beta male, or anything else derogatory for that matter. When a guy speaks negatively about another guy it only goes to highlight that guy's own personal insecurities. So the first "beta" male behaviour you should avoid is using that term. For the same reason you should resist the temptation to speak ill of other people, especially when they're not around to defend themselves. Besides, women always see through this behaviour and they always, always, absolutely always take the side of the guy you're speaking down about. If a guy is no threat to you, then don't act like he is!

Likewise, as the alpha it is your job to call people out on bad behaviour and tell them it's not needed and not respected. Remember you're trying to create that perfect environment for yourself and that means not having to put up with those who're disrespectful. This includes people who're disrespectful to you as well as disrespectful of others.

You should avoid swearing. It shows a lack of refinement among other things, it also shows insecurity and quite possibly a lack of education.

Don't ever put yourself down! We all make mistakes; the difference is the alpha learns from them and moves on, everybody else allows those mistakes to affect them negatively. The only reason you should ever put yourself down is if it's an obvious joke which can even be endearing. Showing self-depreciation when you're an obvious alpha male can be a positive as long as it is a joke.

Don't ever brag about your achievements. If you follow the advice in this book then you're going to be racking up quite a few of them. Learn the difference between telling a story about something cool you've just done such as sky diving and bragging about having just gone sky diving. Besides, if people discover interesting things about you on their own, and not through bragging, it's a hundred times more powerful.

Question: How can I be that guy who everybody just knows is alpha the second he walks in the room?

Answer: Keep your eyes peeled for when these rare specimens enter a coffee shop, bar or anywhere else. Just how do they do it?

For starters they are always dressed well. That is essential! They walk with confidence, with their heads held up. They are slow, controlled and have a calming and trustworthy aura about themselves. What's more they say "Good morning!" to the shop clerk, barista or to others who are around. They speak with a loud and authoritative voice. Confidence! While everybody else in the room is afraid to make small talk, the alpha male is not. They take an interest in making pleasantries to people and asking how they are; the little things. That's all it takes to get noticed in a room where nobody else is even smiling.

If you do everything I've mentioned in this book then people *will* look at you when you walk into the room. At the beginning of this book I mentioned that women regularly approach me when I go to bars for example. The fact I make small talk and make my presence known in a room has a large part to do with that. When you do it, don't do it because you're expecting something in return. Do it because it's who you are!

Question: Is it true that I should be a protector of my friends?

Yes! Like the lion, it is the job of the alpha male to be the protector in the unlikely event there are any problems in your group. If you are the alpha, you will find everybody else will turn to you in a crisis because you are the calm guy who is keeping their head. No, this doesn't mean that you need to use violence to protect your group, but everybody's instincts will be to expect the alpha to diffuse any potentially explosive situations.

In addition, it is the alpha who should be walking closer to the road and your group should be on the inside when you're in the street. This is something you will do automatically when you have a family. You will feel protective over them and so you will naturally place yourself in the path of where the potential danger will come from. Notice this the next time you see a family walking along the street.

Question: How can I out alpha another alpha?

Commonly known as AMOG'ing (Alpha Male Of Group'ing), the key thing is never to feel threatened and to be the calmest guy in the situation. While he's trying to impress your group, you should simply sit back, relax, take up space and allow him to carry on. What's more, you need to allow him to try and impress you. Never try and impress him! It is your approval he needs to seek, not the other way around. If he tells a story, feel free to comment on it, show *your* approval! Compliment him on little things, "I really like your jacket!" This demonstrates even more that you're the approval giver, the one he needs to impress. Finally you should lead your group as usual. The addition of the AMOG shouldn't make a difference to you. Use shoulder taps and back pats. Be aware if he tries any of this on you.

Conclusion

Having the ability to be the alpha male is a skill that many seem to be losing. The media is constantly breaking men down while building women up. While there is nothing wrong with the latter, it will come as no surprise that the rise of the "metro sexual" is becoming detrimental to men as a whole.

Despite leadership being a well sought out quality in the work place and in every day practical situations; men who can naturally take the lead due to an inbuilt complete belief in themselves are becoming extremely rare.

In fact they are so rare in this year of 2012 that any man who demonstrates alpha traits, or simply excellence in the components I mentioned (physical attraction, confidence, ambition, displays of expertise, social proof, leadership, ability to connect, life experience) will be immediately noticeable and desired by the vast majority of women.

Despite the emergence of strong females, taking the place of the strong male in society, women still crave that strong male who is becoming an ever more rare specimen today.

When it really comes down to it, there are no tricks involved in being an alpha male. All I have asked you to do really is to be the best possible person you can be. Why would women not be attracted to that?

I ask you to make an effort with all eight of the alpha elements I laid out in this book. Some will require more work than others, but they are all equally important. Many of them will complement each other and go hand in hand.

Be under no illusion, you cannot become this guy overnight. Think of it as a work in progress. Sure you can fix your body language and your dress sense extremely quickly. But you must also think longer term too. I suggest you begin by doing that one thing you've been wanting to do and have been putting off for years. What is it? A cross country bike ride, a marathon, a qualification, a new skill or even a weekend alone in the forest. Getting out there and experiencing life is a huge fundamental element to being the guy you want to be.

I wish you the best of luck!

The only way to expand your comfort zone is to live outside it!

Charlie Valentino

Also By Charlie Valentino

First Date Tips For Men

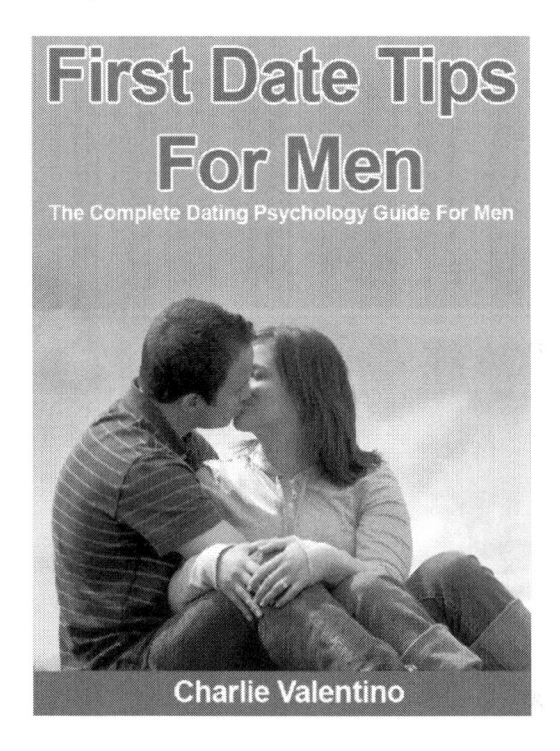

The complete dating psychology guide for men! - This powerful book gives men the ability to completely captivate women on dates.

There are many techniques and strategies in First Date Tips for Men, some practical, others logistical. However it is the psychological tips, the getting into the female mind, to have her thinking about you even after the date is over that really makes this book truly unique.

Here's a few of the things you'll learn inside:

- How to compliment her correctly to get her to open up to you.
- Establishing a connection. This will make her feel like she's known you a long time.
- Rapport breaking. This is powerful and will make her chase you.
- Qualification. This is the secret weapon. Few guys use qualification! This is how you stand out and get her to chase you for a long time.

If only I knew these things as a teenager!

Meet Women On Facebook

meet women on facebook
the ultimate facebook pick up guide

by: charlie valentino

Meeting women on Facebook is easy, as long as you know what you're doing!

You need a profile that makes you stand out from the rest of the guys out there, who message random girls all the time hoping for a response.

Learn how to craft the best Facebook profile possible to enable picking up girls on Facebook easy!

After that, use our Facebook pick up lines to pique her interest and have her impatiently message you back.

It's all here in Meet Women on Facebook to make Facebook pick up easy for any guy out there.

No matter if she's an existing Facebook friend, a friend of a friend or you have no connection with her whatsoever, discover the complete formula from the first message to the first date now.

With most of the world's hot girls on Facebook, Facebook dating is the future! Don't miss the boat on this one!

Confidence For Men

24 Instant Confidence Boosting Tips

by: charlie valentino

This revolutionary book which aims to help men from all walks of life improve their self-confidence contains 24 chapters of easy to implement tips and strategies.

Discover the subtle body language traits which all confident men have and how you can use confident body language to actually fool your brain into thinking you're a confident man.

Learn about becoming a leader, one of the most important things all confident people have in common.

You'll also find out how to create the best possible social circle, the importance of identifying and cutting out negative people who bring you down and instead finding and including those people who'll add to your life.

Building self-confidence to last you the rest of your life begins with taking action! Confidence for Men emphasizes the importance of taking action. That action starts here!

Destroy Approach Anxiety – Effortlessly Approach Women Without Fear

Approach anxiety is something the vast majority of aspiring pick up artists suffer from when starting out approaching girls. If we can't get over approach anxiety, our first major stumbling block in the world of pick up then we're not going to meet many attractive women.

Destroy Approach Anxiety covers this subject so you can get over this easily and then on to the good stuff which is approaching women without fear.

Find out the true reasons why we suffer from approach anxiety, it may surprise you. One of the author's beliefs is that it's the overloading of information in our heads in an attempt to gain perfection before we've even made our first approach. This is impossible!

The author emphasizes the importance of keeping pick up as simple as possible, especially when suffering from approach anxiety. He gives numerous strategies for maintaining the perfect pick up, without overloading the head with too much information, which you can't possibly act on when under pressure approaching hot women.

Destroy Approach Anxiety should be the first PUA book you read as it will help you find approaching girls in the street as simple as possible by getting you in the right frame of mind.

Direct Day Game Method – Pickup Girls on the Street, at the Mall or Coffee Shop!

Direct day game allows guys to cut the crap and just get to the point! It's just you and her in the moment! That's why it works so well, women respect guys who put themselves on the line! - Charlie Valentino.

There is nothing quite so empowering as being able to walk straight up to any girl in the middle of the street and tell her you think she's stunning! This is what Charlie has been doing for years and he shows you how you can do it too.

Using the direct approach on a girl during the day in the street, coffee shop, mall or university campus is about as straightforward as pickup gets. For this reason Charlie Valentino says it's the best method for beginners and newbies or for those suffering from approach anxiety. Because the direct day game approach for meeting women really does cut the structure of pick up right down to its bare bones. There will be no rubbish flying through your head, no lines, stories, routines, tips or tricks. It's just you and a very attractive girl in the moment.

Charlie shows you how it's done with ease and a high probability of success!

Online Dating For Men

Online Dating For Men

Charlie Valentino

1 in 5 new relationships now begin from an online dating site. Given that only a few short years ago this figure was zero, this is quite impressive. It is estimated that within a few years, the vast majority of new relationships will begin through meeting on an online dating site!

Having said that, 95% of all men who sign up to an internet dating site will give up within one subscription term.

Charlie Valentino has now authored his sixth relationship book for men, aiming to help guys meet their dream girl whether on Match.com, Plenty of Fish or any other online dating site.

In this book you'll learn:
- The mind set and strategy you must take to set yourself apart from all the other guys online.
- The pitfalls of online dating and why most men fail.
- The webs best online dating sites and which ones to avoid.
- All you need to know to create the single best profile that will stop women in their tracks. Crafting that perfect profile is the single most important thing you must do to ensure women return your emails. Charlie Valentino previously authored Meet Women on Facebook and is an expert on creating enticing online profiles.
- Discover the many mistakes that men make with their profiles so you can ensure you don't make the same mistakes.
- Learn how to craft the perfect opening email to send to girls to give yourself the highest possible chance of receiving a reply.
- Charlie also shows you his tried and tested cut and paste email system.
- See evidence of what 99% of guys are doing and why it's impossible for them to stand out and make any impact. This is valuable information to know, so you don't do the same.

Online Dating For Men contains all you need to know in order to attract women online, improving dramatically your chances of dating as many women as you like through online dating websites.

Made in the USA
Lexington, KY
25 March 2014